SINISTER

SINISTER

Jimmy James

SINISTER

iUniverse books may be ordered through booksellers or by contacting:

iUniverse
1663 Liberty Drive
Bloomington, IN 47403
www.iuniverse.com
844-349-9409

ISBN: 978-1-6632-0642-8 (sc)
ISBN: 978-1-6632-0643-5 (e)

Library of Congress Control Number: 2024902345

Print information available on the last page.

iUniverse rev. date: 01/30/2024

CONTENTS

DEDICATION

I dedicate this book to my father and mother, who spent their life savings on hospital bills to keep me alive when I was a child and cared for me at home.

CHAPTER ONE

A BLESSING

I started to get more comfortable in the bed and covered up. I felt the hot, humid air of the desert as beads of sweat started to run down my face, and I noticed the back of my father's black and white eagle feather headdress as he drank from Crystal Blue River. He quickly rose to his mighty 6'2" build and stared deeply at me with his brown eyes.

He yelled, "Moccasin Mountain."

Suddenly, I heard a loud crack of thunder as my father pointed his tan left arm toward the lit-up sky in the distance, showing me the path we would take through the valley. I followed each of my father's footprints in the hot pink sand of the desert floor. The thunder got louder and louder with every step we took.

I noticed all the tall, red sandstone cliffs on both sides of us as the sky lit up with mighty lightning bolts, one right after another. The lightning bolts would turn the cliffs into giant grayish cement tombstones. Suddenly, out of nowhere, numerous large brown, dried-up tumbleweeds came rushing at us. Some of the tumbleweeds had a skull in the middle of them as they stopped and taunted me. I stood next to my father, out of breath. As I heard my father say, "The great white fathers," in a basin tone, I observed the light blue sky adorned with four massive white clouds, one of which stood apart from the others.

I glanced over and saw my mother standing on the left side of the cloud. She was dressed in a long, light brown deer skin hide. I quickly went into the spirit and stood beside her, admiring her long, shiny black hair.

As I entered the long tunnel, she slowly pointed her left hand and index finger toward a big, black hole in the white cloud. There was a cave at the end of the tunnel, with people from all different nationalities standing there. They all looked tired and hungry. Some even wore rags for clothes.

My phone started ringing. As the screen lit up, I saw it was Judy calling. Judy was my case manager at the Salvation Army Project Homes. I had lived there for a year. The purpose of Project Homes was to temporarily access, coordinate, and provide supportive services, including shelter, to individuals transitioning to more permanent housing. I'll never forget the first day I met Judy. I was so nervous. I was homeless for two and a half years, and four shelters denied me refuge. This was the last shelter within any surrounding counties.

As she continued explaining the program, I scratched my left forearm absentmindedly. Instead of rent, you paid program fees there, so technically, I would still be classified as homeless. The program fees were calculated at 30% of your gross income, not exceeding $300.00 monthly. I couldn't stop scratching my left forearm. I was scratching so hard and fast that I started to bleed from that area. No drinking, drug use, or smoking was permitted in the building. Overnight guests were also prohibited. Additionally, I would be required to meet with her bi-weekly.

Judy said, "Jimmy, I noticed your car was in the parking lot. Is there some reason you didn't go to work today?"

Rapidly breathing and sitting up in the single bed with a sad look on my face, I let out a sigh. In a sad tone, I said, "Yeah, I'm going to have to talk to you about a few things. Will you have time later for me to come down and talk to you about them?"

She said, "Well, I need to talk to you about something concerning your housing. Do you think you could make it down here within the next 10 minutes?"

I made it to her office. She sympathetically said, "This isn't like you to miss work, Jimmy. Is everything okay? You don't look sick to me."

"I was fired from Wood County Packaging yesterday," I answered.

I handed her the document, which stated that in the last six months, I had missed a day of work and left early 12 times. They wanted me to sign the document, but I would not. I tried to explain that I had permission to leave work early from Slick, but they didn't want to hear it. They knew what they were doing and that it was against the law. I did the right thing and reported Oscar, the supervisor, for sexual harassment in the workplace. Oscar would go around the plant all day rubbing on the women line leaders. You could tell by their faces that they didn't like it one bit. That was the real reason why I was fired.

Eric asked me if I wanted to add anything to the document before he made copies of it. I gladly added, "I'm sick of watching Oscar go around the plant for the last 19 months rubbing up on women line leaders."

I noticed Judy reaching for the blue file on the white calendar and opening it up. She said, "Well, according to your file here, you have been working there for 19 months. I don't see any reason you would have any problem finding another job."

Since living at Project Homes and setting up monthly goals with Judy, I paid off all the bills I accumulated in my early stages of homelessness. There was only one bill that I didn't pay, and that was to the repo man; they wanted all their money at once. My long-term goals were to pay off all my bills, find better employment, work my way off government assistance, write and publish two books, market my books and T-shirts, and make a TV commercial for Project Homes. I was able to accomplish writing and publishing Fracas within a year.

I found my resume and looked it over. I confidently thought, *I really don't think I'm going to have a problem finding employment with a resume like this.* I crossed my legs and thought, *You know, the system is broken for people like me. I paid my debt to society. All I'm trying to do is make an honest living.*

Judy was a very professional businesswoman and took her job very seriously. She stared at me and intelligently said, "Well, I remember you telling me during your interview to get in here that when you were released from prison, you used to put in five applications a day until you found employment." She reached for a monthly goal sheet and continued, "You're going to have to make up some new goals for yourself." She grabbed her blue pen, "I think your first goal should be to put in three to five applications daily until you find employment. Are there any other goals you should add to this list?"

One of my monthly goals for the last year was to find better employment. Nobody was calling me, and I knew it was all because of the criminal background check. I had another paycheck coming, but it was only for six days of work. I already did the math before I came down to talk with Judy. After paying my monthly program fees, I would only have $100.00 left. I would have to devise a plan to receive money from unemployment. However, I knew it would take a few weeks before I would start to receive unemployment benefits.

I answered Judy, "Yeah, call unemployment."

Judy wrote down the goals.

I said, "Call Debbie and let her know I won't be volunteering at the shelter anymore."

When I left the shelter to move into Project Homes, I signed up to volunteer. They did a lot for me. They found me employment and even allowed me to live on their floor past the required time frame. I volunteered every Sunday at 4:00 a.m. I was responsible for finishing up the laundry and serving breakfast. It wasn't that hard, and it was only for a few hours every Sunday morning. I would have everything put away in the kitchen and cleaned up with time to spare before the shelter closed for the morning.

As she continued to write, she looked up at me and asked, "Do you want me to put anything down about the books?"

"Yeah, I'm going to keep writing," I answered. "You know, it's starting to seem like every time I publish a book, I get fired from a job."

She stopped writing and leaned back in her chair. She said, "Well, that's not true. When you were staying down at the shelter, you wrote a book and published it, and Wood County Packaging didn't fire you then!"

I bit my bottom lip briefly and replied, "Well, they did want to lay me off last year. They didn't because Gail and Slick knew I was a good worker and went to bat for me. Look at when I worked for the bakery in Milltown; I published *A Line 2 Die 4*, and a few weeks later, I was fired with no write-ups in my work file. Now I publish another book, and Wood County Packaging fires me."

Judy said, "Jimmy, I called you down today because I have some bad news for you. Do you remember when I signed you up for Wood County Housing? Well, they're not accepting new clients for the rest of the year."

Wood County Housing was for low-income people who needed assistance with housing. They would pay up to 30% of your rent based on your income.

She continued, "Wood County Housing informed me that you would be eligible for housing at the beginning of next year."

I nodded my head back and forth and responded, "That's just fucking great! Are we done here?"

As I stood up and started to walk out of her office, I heard, "See you in two weeks with your monthly budget form."

I laid in bed with so many thoughts—the books, unemployment, employment, housing, volunteering, and repo man. For some odd reason, I started to think about what happened to Steve Urban. I never met the person, but when I was caged up like an animal, I would hear the name come up from time to time. In the 1980s, a person with a life sentence (lifer) would serve, on average, 13-15 years before release on parole. In the 1970s, it was much shorter because Wisconsin governors routinely granted clemency to lifers by commuting their sentences to 50 years or less. This allowed lifers to receive parole hearings far before the statutorily mandated 11 years, three months (one lifer had his sentence commuted to "time served" after only five years).

It was so rare for a lifer to spend more than 20 consecutive years in prison that in 1980, there were only two prisoners with that distinction. In 1990, it was newsworthy when Steve Urban died in prison after serving 47 years on a life sentence. He was released on parole in the early 1970s, but by then, he had become institutionalized and quickly demanded that he be allowed to return to prison. When he died, he had no family to claim his body, which was buried in a pauper's grave outside Waupun. The Waupun Correctional Institution Lifers Group took up a collection and bought a headstone for his grave.

I was a survivor. I wasn't going out like that. I quickly got out of bed and called unemployment. I heard that busy signal over and over. I stared at the Employee Corrective Action Plan pinned up on the bulletin board in the kitchen and started to read it. It said, "Explanation of Offense (be specific): Jimmy causes problems on every line we put him on. He constantly complains about wages and work conditions and disrespects the supervisors. He loudly tries to rally the other employees to turn against the company. He refuses to stay quiet and make the rate on the jobs we put him on. It has gotten to the point where none of the supervisors want him on their line."

I glanced down at the action to be taken and noticed it escalated straight to a final warning. They never gave me a verbal warning. I knew I couldn't fight that for one minute. There was no verbal warning, no written warning, and no 3-day suspension; it just went straight to a final warning. They had no paper trail at all. They didn't even follow their own protocol in their handbook. I pressed redial on the phone while reading the employees' comments section.

When Eric returned with a copy of the document that day and handed it to me, I read the employee correction action plan. He had falsified the document.

He wrote, "During the meeting, Jimmy said he wanted to get fired to collect unemployment and would win the case he always does."

He didn't even sign his whole name after the little comment he added to the document. He also wrote, "I don't know. I had been in management for years and never heard anyone say that to me when they were getting fired. And why would they even say something like that?"

I told him right to his face that he falsified the document, it was against the law, and that I was going to the human resource department.

I heard him yell, "I'm going fight your unemployment all the way."

Everyone working on the production floor stopped what they were doing.

I heard the unemployment operator ask, "Name and social security number, please?" I gave her the information and answered all questions that were required. I was curious; I wanted to know what she thought about a few things.

I took a deep breath and asked, "How long do you think it will be before I get an unemployment check?"

She replied, "Well, sir, it could take 3 to 4 weeks before you see an unemployment check."

Scratching my head with my right hand, I said, "Let me ask you this. They say I walked off the job, but I didn't. I notified two supervisors that I would talk to the Human Resource Department."

She stared at her computer screen and respectfully said, "Sir, I'm just a claims specialist, but they have the right to dispute the claim you filed today."

My phone started to buzz; it was Rubio. I remember the first time I met her. It was 11 years ago. I was locked up doing hard time in the State pen. Gravedog, a biker I used to sell drugs to, told Juan, the leader of the

Tri-City Bombers, that Rubio was a very trustworthy person. Juan checked her out and gave her the blessing she needed. I didn't even know what she looked like, but she was on my visiting list. She would come every Monday like clockwork.

The first time I saw her, I knew why Juan called her Rubio, meaning blonde in Spanish, because she sure had a lot of blonde in her. The one thing I liked about Rubio was that she was very respectable. When our visits were up, she ensured all the trash was picked up and tossed into a certain garbage container.

Tony, one of my "vatos," worked in the kitchen, and he knew what garbage can he had to empty. That's how we got the drugs into the prison system and how the Tri-City Bombers made their rice and beans in the joint.

Rubio and I became tight; we clicked the first time we met. Even after I was released from prison, we remained friends. But since her daughter Tia was released from prison and on extended supervision, we didn't see each other as much as we used to. We kept in touch but only through text messages.

The message read, "What did Judy say about you being fired?"

I replied, "She said I have to look for at least five jobs daily. I still have another check coming for six days of pay. I'm all good for another month here."

Rubio had Tia's PO lock up Tia to do a drug and alcohol program, and she was coming home today.

Rubio responded, "Everything is going to work out for you. I have to go. Tia and the PO just got here."

I called Debbie to give her the heads up. Debbie was the volunteer coordinator for the shelter. She would go all over the place to find volunteers—churches, fundraisers, PTA Meetings, you name it; Debbie was there and did a good job at it. The shelter always had volunteers coming in to help out. Sometimes, they had too many volunteers coming in, but Debbie always found something for them to do, and they enjoyed doing it.

When I was leaving the shelter that day to move into Project Homes, Debbie approached me and asked if I wanted to come back to the shelter to volunteer. I was honored. I said, "Yeah, why not?" I had to pay my debt back somehow. This place saved me when there was no other place. Debbie really made my day when she asked me. She had also asked a few other clients to come back after they left the shelter, but she stopped doing that because the few she asked didn't turn out how she expected. Some clients she asked would come in drunk or not even come in at all.

Debbie asking me to be part of the shelter hit me down deep inside. I would be part of something, and that something would be good in my life. This is what I really needed to keep me going. Judy even thought it was a good idea for me to go to the shelter and volunteer every Sunday morning.

I called Debbie, and it went straight to voicemail. I left a message saying I could volunteer the upcoming Sunday morning but not the following Sunday. I knew Debbie wouldn't have a problem filling my slot. That Sunday morning, when I was volunteering for the last time, Al walked up to me in the kitchen. Al was promoted to case manager when Raine left. I guess she just got into her canoe with her pit bull, Oliver, last week and started paddling her way down the Fox River. She didn't know where she was going; it was just like how she ended up at the shelter.

Raine came ashore one day in her canoe to get some supplies. That's when she spotted this pit bull barking at a guy who was cornered in the back of this alley. The dog was ready to attack him. Raine slowly walked up to the pit bull and gave him a piece of Beef Jerky, and a few seconds later, she pulled a splinter of wood out of the dog's right back paw. Dick was the person who the dog had cornered. He offered Raine the assistant director position at the shelter that day.

Raine worked for the shelter for just over two years during that time. She helped out 1,114 homeless people, including 78 women and 104 veterans. Out of the 1,114, she found refuge for all of them. She sent them to different types of organizations that were set up in Wood County.

While I was staying in the shelter, she once told me, "You're like a small tuft of grass growing through a crack in the concrete. It's incredibly heroic."

Al had some big shoes to fill. Standing on the other side of the 4 x 12 stainless steel table, he asked, "Could you stay late after the shelter closes? Dick and I would like to talk with you about something."

Dick was the director of the shelter. He was a millionaire. I heard through the grapevine that he had an aunt he never met who died and left him all this money. His job duties were to raise money for the shelter since it opened. The shelter only allowed a stay of up to six months, and that was it. There was a waiting list to get into Project Homes. Dick told me I could stay as long as it took me to get into Project Homes. It was a long seven and a half months sleeping on that floor.

"Have a seat at the table, Jimmy," Al said, "Dick will be with us in a minute."

I noticed Dick walking toward us on the shiny, clean white tile floor with his 6'4 and skinny 180-pound body.

"What's going on, Jimmy?" he asked as we shook hands. "Debbie called me yesterday, saying that you can't volunteer anymore and will most likely have to come back to the shelter to sleep. What's going on?"

I made eye contact with his green eyes and said, "Well, I was fired from Wood County Packaging about a week ago, and I don't have any money to pay program fees at Project Homes. Judy said everything would be okay, but I've been down this road before."

He sat down next to me, with his red hair and goatee matching. He said, "Well, since Raine left the shelter, the client numbers have been increasing, and we have been thinking about adding another person to the overnight shift. Would you be interested in something like this?"

My upper eyelids rose as I looked at Al and heard, "The only thing is that you would have to work the overnight shifts. Would that be a problem?"

I nodded my head back and forth. "No, I can work the overnight shifts. When would I start?"

Al started to get up out of his chair. He said, "All you have to do is fill out some basic paperwork, and you could start next Monday. I'll be right back with the paperwork that needs to be filled out."

Looking over at Dick, I asked, "Are you sure about this? I mean, don't get me wrong here. I need a job, but I'm not trained in any of this."

He got up from his chair and looked down at me through his glasses. "You're trained already. Let me put it this way. If you needed an operation, would you go to a person who read about the operation, or would you go to the person who has done the operation already? Jimmy, I want you to be a mentor here."

Al sat beside me and said, "Yeah, you're all trained already because you have lived it, plus the clients respect you. All you have to do is learn the computer stuff, which will come in time. Here you go; complete the paperwork and return it when you're done. If I'm not here, just leave it with whoever is working here that night."

When I got to my car, I texted Rubio, "Hey, you're not going to believe this one. The shelter just hired me to work full-time. Al and Dick said I'm all trained already; I just need to learn some of the paperwork."

My phone buzzed; it was Rubio. "I'm happy for you, but how did you pull that off?"

I lit up a smoke and texted back, "I don't know. After I was done volunteering, Al and Dick asked me if I would like to work there. My hours are 11:00 pm to 7:00 am."

"How much are they paying you?"

I started my car and replied, "I'm making $2 more than I was at WCP."

"Are they still hiring?"

I placed the car in reverse and quickly texted her, "I don't know. When I hand in the paperwork they gave me to fill out, I'll check on it."

"Are you still coming to Tia's intervention next Wednesday?"

"Yeah, I'll be there. She needs all the support she can get. I'm going home to fill out all of this paperwork and hand it in."

When I got back to my room, I started filling out the paperwork Al gave me. What a blessing! I would start work two weeks to the date after Wood County Packaging fired me, with a $2.00 raise on top of it.

* * *

It was my first night working at the shelter. I had to work with this guy named Chicken Nugget. I'd never met him before. I knew some of the clients didn't like him.

Al called me early in the day to make sure I was coming in. He filled me in a little bit about Chicken Nugget on the phone. He was like a military brat. He never joined the military, but his father was, and they moved around the world. Everything was right down to the minute with him. They called him Chicken Nugget because he would stop at a fast food joint every night he worked at the shelter and buy chicken nuggets and two other sandwiches.

Al also told me on the phone that Bobbie and Thrifty would be there until he showed up for his shift at midnight. I had met Bobbie once before when I turned all my paperwork in. She's the one who gave me all the work keys for the shelter. Bobbie was attending college in the social work field. She was a White woman in her mid-twenties with a dark tan complexion, blue eyes, and long blonde hair. Raine hired Bobbie to be the assistant case manager for the shelter because Tim had left the shelter to run his own group home for at-risk children.

Bobbie waved at me from behind the bulletproof glass as I entered the lobby. I used my key card to unlock the lobby door and immediately headed for the small 10 x 12 office so I wouldn't disturb any clients sleeping. I slowly closed the maple door behind me.

Bobbie said, "Hi, Jimmy. Have you met Thrifty?"

I glanced over at him sitting in the chair. I said, "No," as I nodded back and forth. I waited for him to get out of the chair, in his 6'3" frame, to shake my hand. He just nodded his short brown hair and head at me. As he started to bitch about the shelter and how it was running, I said, "I was hired by Raine to do service point and only service point."

I told Al that I wouldn't do service point if he needed me to type up his notes in the shift report.

Bobbie continued to type on the gray keyboard. She said, "Raine hired me as an assistant case manager. When she left, I should've been promoted to her position, not Al; he doesn't even know how to type, and I'm not going to be his secretary either!"

Turning around in her chair with the work schedule in her hand, she said, "Al told me to give you the work schedule as soon as you come in." She showed me how the work schedule works. "You'll be working with Chicken Nugget tonight."

I heard both of them start to chuckle at the same time. Thrifty said, "Boy or boy, do you have a long night ahead of you!" He sat next to the security camera monitor and continued, "Chicken Nugget is another one who doesn't have a clue on how this place should be run." He struggled to get up from his worn-down, 220-pound body. "I need to get out of here before he shows up." He limped out of the office. He was sort of bow-legged.

Bobbie showed me how to do a head count. She counted the names in the book, then went out and took a physical head count of the clients sleeping on the floor. After the count, she showed me where to document it.

She said, "When working with Chicken Nugget tonight, don't let him tell you how to treat the clients. I hear from the clients all the time how he treats them."

When he entered the office, I saw he was a short White boy with a 5'1 and 235-pound body. He had short dark hair and wore glasses. He had a bag of fast food in his hands.

Chicken Nugget said, "Hey, what's up? You must be Jimmy?"

I got out of the chair to shake his hand. As we shook hands, Bobbie started to fill him in on what happened at the shelter. After Bobbie left, he just sat there eating his fast food. With his mouth full of food, he asked, "Did you get a chance to meet Thrifty tonight?"

I crossed my legs and answered, "Yeah, he was here when I came in tonight."

Feeding his face, Chicken Nugget said, "I'm surprised he didn't try to sell you any of his junk. All he does is go from one thrift store to the next trying to find junk that he can sell on his website, but the funny thing is he won't hand out the web address to anyone at work." He took a sip of his soda and continued, "The only reason Raine hired him was because he worked at this other shelter further up north. He said he's been working at a shelter for two years, but the shelter where he worked only opened up for six months out of a year."

As we sat watching all the clients sleep, he told me how I should act around the clients. He stated in a strict tone, "They have to fear you; that's the only way they will respect you."

I looked over at him as he sat in front of the lit-up computer screen. I said, "I don't know about that. I sold drugs for over 26 years, and one of the things I learned on the streets was to show respect to get respect. That always worked for me."

He turned his head and sharply looked at me. "Well, you're going to find out the hard way! It doesn't work like this here with the clients. I've been working here for four months now. Either you're going to follow my lead, or else I'm going to tell Dick and Al that you don't fit in here!"

I quickly got out of the gray leather chair and looked down at him. I said, "I'm going outside to smoke, and you can tell Dick and Al whatever you want. They both told me when they hired me that I was already trained and I should be a mentor to the clients since I've been homeless for over three years."

As I left the office, I heard, "I was homeless once in my life!"

I didn't believe a word he said because he wouldn't have been trying to make the clients fear him if he had been homeless once.

Later that morning, we had a few wake-up calls. Four clients had to be up early to go to work. I asked the volunteer in the kitchen to set out breakfast for the workers. It was just some hard-boiled eggs, cereal, and coffee. When they were done eating, one of the clients who knew me from when I used to sleep on the floor said, "I heard a rumor a few days ago that you're not a volunteer anymore and that you're working here now."

I answered, "Yeah, I'm working here now."

He smiled as he stood in the lobby waiting for the silver tray with his bag lunch to open. In a cocky tone, he yelled, "Hey, I'm running late, I need my lunch!"

Chicken Nugget jumped out of his chair and yelled back, "I don't have to give you a bag lunch."

I jumped into the conversation quickly, saying, "What do you mean the shelter doesn't have to give him a bag lunch?"

Chicken Nugget held his ground. "It's not written in any rules that we have to feed a client!"

I got out of the chair as the two argued over the bag lunch. I said, "Hey, I'll be right back."

I went into the kitchen, grabbed all the lunches made up by the volunteer, and brought them into the office. I gave the client one. He asked, "Jimmy, do you have a minute to talk?"

I stepped out into the lobby. The guy continued, "He does this to us every morning. Why would a person want to work at a shelter if he doesn't want to help us? It's not like it's coming out of his pocket if he gives us a lunch."

I took a deep breath and looked over at him. "You don't have to worry about that anymore. I'm going to be working the overnight shifts from now on. I'll make sure you guys get your lunches without any problems."

It was 7:00 a.m., and time for me to go home. A few hours later, I texted Rubio. "Hey, I got my work schedule last night at work. I have a staff meeting on the day of Tia's intervention. I won't be able to make it. Sorry."

Rubio replied, "Well, that sucks! I was really counting on you showing up and telling Tia some of your story and how you are making it. How was your first night at work?"

I responded, "I really liked it. I think they are still looking for more people to hire because I saw a few open spots on the schedule. I even have to work by myself on Wednesday night."

"Can you pick me up an app?"

<hr/>

The following night, I was working with Stephanie. She talked most of the night away. Stephanie had worked at the shelter shortly before I had stayed there. When Raine became the assistant director, she fired Stephanie a few weeks later. Al and Dick hired her back just a few days before.

Stephanie was an African American woman with long painted fingernails and long, black, shoulder-length dreadlocks. She went to college and had three degrees in social services. She walked right out during the client session at her last job and never returned. She didn't respect people at all. She started to talk about some of the people who worked at the shelter. She said Al wouldn't be there much longer; he was in way over his head. She also said that she and Bobbie would be taking over soon because no one else could do the job.

What puzzled me was that when I arrived at work tonight, Thrifty was telling Bobbie that she needed to speak with a board member to inform them about what Al was doing. Thrifty even mentioned that he and Bobbie would take over the shelter. I could tell by how she talked about Thrifty that the two didn't get along. According to her, Thrifty was the dumbest person in any room he entered. She said he even tried to go to a university but didn't graduate, and all he does is talk about people behind their backs.

She didn't do any wakeup calls or hand out bag lunches to the clients going to work, so I did it all. There were no issues with me handing out the lunches, and all the clients thanked me. Before I knew it, it was 6:00 a.m. I turned on the lights and the two 42-inch flat-screen TVs as the clients started to get up to eat. As I walked around the floor, I stopped to talk with four clients I knew from when I used to sleep on the floor. They were thankful that I was working there. One client said, "It's about time they hired someone to treat us with dignity and respect around here."

Just then, Stephanie came out of the office. I couldn't believe what she did and said. She said, "Look at my new tennis shoes. I just bought them yesterday."

A few clients exclaimed, "See what I'm talking about!"

I just walked away, nodding my head back and forth. I thought, *Why would someone brag about what they have in front of a bunch of homeless people down on their luck?* Suddenly, out of nowhere, a client approached me, asking, "Did you used to sleep on the floor here?"

I looked at him and said, "Yeah, I slept on the floor for over seven months; why?"

He was a short person, maybe 5'2 and 125 pounds. He stared at me with his brown eyes. "Well, you're the person I want to talk to. You made it out of here. How did you do it?"

I took a deep breath and said, "Well, the first thing I did was get a job. Are you working?"

He said, "No, but I have been filling out all kinds of applications everywhere. I never had a hard time finding a job, but now I have a criminal record, and it seems like nobody even wants to look at me. By trade, I'm a certified welder."

I had been in his shoes before. The criminal record leads to homelessness in a lot of cases.

"I know a place that will hire you, and I might be able to hook you up with a landlord," I said. "The place is in Huntsville. Would you have a problem moving to Huntsville?"

We started to walk toward the office. He answered, "Hell no! Anything is better than this."

I grabbed the application for Rubio to fill out and a piece of paper from the desk. "I'm just going to make a note here for when I get off work. I'll do some checking on this for you. I'll see you tomorrow morning and let you know what I came up with, okay?"

⋅⟡⟡⟡⟡⟡⋅

I got out of my car and thought about having to work alone that night. I walked into the office and noticed Bella standing in the office in her 5'8 and 165-pound body, with long blonde hair. I closed the door behind me. Thrifty and Bobbie listened as Bella continued to talk. She said, "Dick came down to the gas station where I was working last night and asked me if I would come back to the shelter to work. Something about the numbers is going up with the clients since Raine left, and they are looking for someone to start helping Al set things up. I don't know what you guys all think about Al running the shelter, but I think he's in way over his head." She looked over at me and said, "Hey, Jimmy, Dick told me that I would be working with you tonight and that you have been working down here for a few days now. How do you like it?"

I nodded and said, "I like it so far. When Dick and Al hired me, they told me I would be a good mentor to the clients because I had lived it."

Bobbie jumped into the conversation, saying, "I believe once he learns all the paperwork, he'll be trained, and I'm going to be training him on the paperwork in a few days."

She turned around in her chair, facing the computer, and continued, "Back to what we were talking about, Bella. You're exactly right! Al is in way over his head. The client numbers just keep on going up. The ten o'clock head count is at 45; I've never seen it this bad." Her right index finger clicked on the gray mouse to send off the shift report. "I talked to Donald just last week about everything happening down here. I also told him that I was done being Al's secretary. He's just going to have to learn how to type."

Donald was the president of the shelter. He was a deep believer in his faith. Before he opened up the shelter, he used to go to prisons, trying to spread the word to inmates. Thrifty put his two cents in as he turned around to face us, "The number of clients coming into the shelter has gotten so bad that I quit entering them into service point. That's Al's fault if he doesn't know how to do services point." They both started to grab their personal items before leaving for the night.

I said, "I think you should talk to Donald again, Bobbie. Tell him what I think happened with Al and a female client tonight. I really think that he's hitting on female clients down here."

After they both left, I went out and did a physical head count. I knew how important it was in case there was an emergency. For example, if a fire broke out, you wouldn't want to send a firefighter in to look for someone who was already outside and risk the firefighter getting hurt inside. When I returned to the office and counted the names in the client log-in book, the count was on. I sat down in the chair; Bella tried to come up with an idea of how working clients should receive their lunches. I told her that Chicken Nugget and I argued the first night. I worked with him over client lunches.

I stared out at the dark, lonely room and watched the clients sleep. Bella said, "Well, I called Stephanie before I came into work tonight, and she said the same thing that Thrifty and Bobbie said about this Chicken Nugget character—that he's a real piece of work." She opened the maple cabinet above her head and checked the work schedule. "Well, I see that

I will be working with him on Friday and Saturday this weekend. He better not even try to pull any crap like that with me! Let's see who you all work with for the rest of the week." She moved her finger to the right on the schedule and continued, "Thursday with Thrifty, Bobbie, and Al. Tomorrow with Klazina." She laughed. "She's the one who replaced me when Raine fired me."

Raine fired Bella because she told clients about a Hippie condo out in Portland, Oregon. I knew Klazina from when I slept on the floor. I never had any problems with her or any other staff when I stayed on the floor.

Bella continued, "Thrifty told me tonight that Klazina told him Al put her in charge."

Klazina was working the morning that I flew out to New York to pitch my books to Hollywood to see if they would make a movie out of them.

I said, "Yeah, she called me into the office that morning before I left. We both got down on our knees, and she said a prayer for me. I didn't think I would have a problem working with her. Even when I was volunteering, we got along just fine.

The following night, Klazina and I sat in the office, and she asked, "Have you noticed anyone putting stuff in my mailbox, Jimmy?"

I looked over at her. "Not really, why?"

She raised her hands and said, "Well, ever since Thrifty started to work here, he's been putting stuff in people's mailboxes. That's his way of telling people they need to be fired or will be fired. I know it's him because I looked back on the security camera."

I noticed someone walking up to the front door on the security camera.

She turned around, facing the computer, and asked, "Have you done an intake on a client yet?"

"No, I have not done an intake on a client, but I have been through the process a few times as a client."

She grabbed the mouse and said, "Come on over here, and I'll walk you through it and see what you know."

She showed me the three major background checks that had to be performed before a client could enter the shelter. When she was done showing me all of that, she pointed to the closet and said, "Go in the closet over there and get a blue intake folder." She placed some personal information in the folder and handed me the intake folder. "Here you go, your first intake. It's all self-explanatory."

I took a deep breath. "Well, like they say, the more you know, the better off you are."

The intake process took about 45 minutes. There were three release forms for the client to sign and the intake itself, which asked a lot of personal questions. After the intake was done, the client received two bins and found a spot to sleep. Klazina reviewed the intake and said, "You did a good job on it. I think you're going to work out just fine here."

That morning, I found the client who had approached me the previous morning about the welding job. I gave him the company phone number and told him they were hiring welders. I also gave him the phone number of the old landlord, where I used to live in Huntsville, who would be willing to work with him on rent and deposit. He lit up like a Christmas tree with this big-ass smile.

I said, "The only problem I see is how in the hell are you going to get up there."

He gave me a high five and said, "As soon as I'm done eating breakfast, I'm going to take a few blankets and ride my bike up there. All I need is to get hired, and I'll have my own place again. Thank you so much. You're a lifesaver."

Since this was my first night shift, Al asked, "How's it going on the overnight shift? Do you like the job?"

I answered, "Yeah, I like the job, and the clients look up to me. I even found a client a job and housing yesterday."

He smiled. "I told you that you would be good at this, didn't I?"

I felt good down deep inside. I did something good for someone who was down on his luck. I said, "Hey, I heard a rumor in the office that you're leaving the shelter. What's up with that?"

He tilted his head to the right and let out a sigh. "Well, do you remember when you were living on the floor here, and I asked you about the prison system and how it was inside? Well, I've been thinking about it. Ever since that day, I decided to go for it. But there are a few things I have to do before I leave. Maybe you could help me out with one of them. Do you know anyone looking for a job?"

"Well, I know Rubio has been thinking about getting a job," I replied. "Do you remember Rubio from when I gave the speech that night?"

Wearing a grin from ear to ear, he exclaimed, "That sexy hot blonde who used to let you sleep on her couch on the weekends when you were homeless? Yeah, call her and see if she wants to work here. If she says yes, give her my phone number and tell her to call me. Oh, yeah, good job finding employment and housing for one of the clients."

I immediately texted Rubio to see if she had filled out the application to work at the shelter. I gave her Al's phone number in case she did.

Al and I walked into the office. "Bobbie, please do me a favor and show Jimmy all the paperwork you do on the night shift."

She smiled beautifully and said, "Yes, I can do that."

She showed me everything. The first thing was the Spreadsheet, which is a daily list of clients staying at the shelter. For every night a client stayed, you had to put an X for that day. If clients were gone for over three consecutive days on the spreadsheet, their bins would be recycled. The bedding bins were placed back by the washer and dryer to be washed. The clients' personal property was placed into a big, clear plastic bag with their name on it and taken downstairs into the basement.

The guest master list had some of the clients' personal information, such as their name, intake number, birthday, the day they came into the shelter, if they were on probation or parole, and if they were registered sex offenders. She showed me how to make up intake folders. Red was for women, and blue was for men.

It was five o'clock, and the clients started to enter the shelter. Bobbie and I checked them in while Thrifty just sat in the office; he didn't interact with the clients all night. The clients seemed to get along with Bobbie, especially the male clients. They would talk about her to me in the mornings. She was one hot sexy bitch. Some clients came in two sheets to the wind. Al had to deal with those clients, as other clients came in perfectly straight.

After the line of clients disappeared, I went out to talk with some clients to see how I could help them. Many asked if I could hook them up with jobs. After all the mats were out, I sat in the office. Thrifty only made it out of the office once to eat. I asked him, "What are you doing on the computer?"

He turned his head and looked over at me. "I'm doing what they call service point. This is how they track homeless people in the State of Wisconsin. Have you been trained on an intake yet?" I nodded. "Well, there's a lot of information on the intake form that needs to be correct in order to do service point. Do you want to learn how to do it?"

I rolled my way over to him. "Well, you know what they say; the more you know, the better off you are."

As he grabbed an intake file from the active filling cabinet, he pointed at what needed to be entered into the computer. "That's it! Nothing to it."

I stared at the computer screen and then at the intake form and thought, *Well, it all makes sense to me now. I wondered why we had to ask some of these questions on the intake form; now I know.*

Bobbie walked into the office, and Thrifty started to bitch up a storm. "Al told me that service point got a hold of him today, and they are asking him why there hasn't been any documentation done in the last two months. So, Al wants me to give out the password to Chicken Nugget so he can start to do service point. I'm not going to do it; it's against the law. If they find out that I gave out my password, they will cut me from service point."

Thrifty looked at Bobbie and said, "You need to talk to Donald again and tell him everything that Al is doing down here is all screwed up and that you and I should be in charge and running the place."

She wore that beautiful smile and said, "I'm going to talk with him again. Al has no training in this field at all. I'm sick of doing his work and not getting paid for it. I graduated from college to be a social worker, and here I am, working for someone with only a GED!"

I got up out of the chair and walked out of the office. I thought, *I don't even have a GED. How would they treat me if they knew that?* I was a high school dropout back in the late 70s. It was my choice, but Juan played a big part in that choice. Juan was the leader of the Tri-City Bombers, the gang I used to kick it with for 26 years. A few months back, I heard through the grapevine that Juan met his match. I guess some young vato named Reyes and five of his vatos jumped him outside the Long Horn Saloon one night and gave him a Cuban necktie. It was payback from when Juan ordered a green light on Reyes' father, Crisco, 22 years earlier.

It was the night before little Reyes' 7th birthday, and Crisco was just out having a good time with his vatos in the Longhorn Saloon. Crisco was stepping up big time. His cousin from Texas came up for the birthday party and brought him a shipment of drugs. Juan wasn't happy about that, but what really kicked the whole thing off was when Crisco pulled out a toy BB gun and pointed it at Juan. He said, "Listen to me when I'm talking to you." Everybody in the club started laughing at Juan, but only for a few seconds.

CHAPTER TWO

SHOT CALLER

I had my bi-weekly meeting with Judy. You should've seen her face when I told her I was working at the shelter as a Night Safety Manager. I said, "Even better, I found a client a job and housing at the same time." Her mouth opened wide. I continued, "I learned to do all the computer stuff and even did an intake, which didn't make sense to me at first, but after Thrifty showed me how to do service point, it all clicked."

She was happy for me and said, "I told you something would come along for you eventually. I know you've been in management before, but you'll be dealing with clients with mental health issues. If you ever need to talk to me about any problems you might encounter with any clients, you know my door is always open."

I looked over at her and scratched my head. "I was hoping you would say something like that. It seems like none of the staff members I work with get along with each other. All they do is complain, and they all want to be the boss of the shelter."

She pulled out a goal sheet. "I'll help you with any problems you have with clients at the shelter, but when it comes to co-workers, you're on your own."

I was back on track with my bi-weekly goals, maybe even better. The shelter gave me a dollar raise after my 30-day probation period. I was making $3.00 more an hour than at Wood County Packaging. I had several goals. The first was to win my unemployment case against Wood County Packaging. I already knew I would win the unemployment case because they didn't even follow their own protocol in the handbook. Another goal was to start saving money for housing. I also wanted to keep working on my next book, and finally, my last goal was to keep employment and start setting things up at the shelter to move clients forward.

The word spread fast in the shelter about me hooking up that client with a job and housing. As a result, about ten to twelve clients asked me daily to hook them up with employment and housing. I told them all to write down the kind of job they were looking for. That's when I came up with the employment book, which I updated daily when finding jobs for them.

Roughly 95% of our clients had no vehicle or valid driver's license, so transportation jobs were out.

Clients couldn't work the third shift either because they wouldn't have a place to sleep. The employment book also had a copy of temporary services, addresses, and phone numbers. I'd go to Craigslist and other job sites, make copies of jobs, and place them in the employment book. I also set up the F-Set program, which took me a few nights. I made out a spreadsheet and went through all the active files.

To qualify for the F-Set Program, the client had to be signed up with Food Share. Two buses arrived at the F-Set Program. Bus 1 arrived at a quarter past the hour, while Bus 30 arrived at a quarter of the hour. The F-Set Program opened at 9:00 a.m. Upon arrival, the receptionist provided the client with their case manager's name and phone number, allowing them to schedule an interview date with the case manager. After the client signed up, they received help with building a resume and cover letter. The client needed to look for employment for at least two hours daily. Each client was given 10 bus passes and required to seek full or part-time employment and keep documentation of their job search to receive more bus passes.

At the F-Set program, there were days when they conducted open interviews, and the client could be employed on the day of the interview.

If the client secured employment, they were given $5.00 cab passes. The client was required to give the cab company a two-hour notice before pick up at their job or the shelter.

I had the F-Set program going for a week, and three of the four clients I sent down came back with employment. I wasn't the only person setting things up at the shelter. Bobbie and Bella did come up with a new way to work with clients on receiving their lunches. A client didn't have to come to the staff anymore to put all the information on the chalkboard. Instead, the document was placed on a clipboard and on one of the tables outside the office. On the document, the working clients could choose the following options: name, save spot, wake-up time, and lunch.

Al called me, wanting to discuss a few things going on at the shelter. He wanted to know if he hired Rubio and a client hit on her, how I'd react since we were close, and Rubio is a very good-looking woman.

I said, "I would shut it down big time, just like any other women staff working at the shelter."

"Good answer," he said, "I'm going to hire her, and she can start work on the overnight shift with you on Tuesday. I will schedule her to work the night shifts if she likes it. I will be cutting Thrifty's hours to only five hours a week. The only reason Raine hired him was to do service point. I just got off the phone with them before I called you, and they told me that Thrifty is now cut from service point because he leaked information. I don't know what I'm going to do with the guy. He keeps sending Bobbie down to Donald to tell him I don't know what I'm doing down here. This isn't the first time he had Bobbie go down and talk with Donald."

I did the right thing because I had nothing to hide. It wasn't my fault that Thrifty showed me how to do services point. I said, "The leak for service point was when Thrifty showed me how to do it one night. I had my bi-weekly meeting with Judy at Project Homes one week later. I told her that Thrifty showed me how to do service point."

He paused on the phone for a few seconds. "You mean he showed you how to do services point? I've been asking him to give Chicken Nugget the password so he could help get caught up on service point. This guy doesn't do a single thing I ask him to do. I'm making the schedule right now. Do you have a problem working Sunday through Wednesday on the overnight shifts and Thursday on the night shift?"

Sunday night, as soon as I walked into the office, Chicken Nugget told me there was a leak in service point, and Thrifty was cut off. He remarked, "What a dumb ass! He wouldn't give me the password to help him, but he leaked information. He even went on Wisconsin CCAP, looked up your criminal record, and told all the staff over the weekend that you shouldn't be working here. Did you really blow someone up when you were in a ~~gang~~?"

I took a deep breath and replied, "No, I didn't blow anyone up, and it's none of Thrifty's business what I did in my past. I paid my debt to society, and the shelter knows about my past."

He reached for the phone, saying, "Thrifty got into a whole lot of arguments with staff over the weekend over it. I guess Al cut his hours down to five hours a week. Oh, yeah, the 12 to 4 volunteer isn't coming in tonight."

I looked at him and asked, "What's the procedure when a volunteer doesn't show up?"

He turned sharply. "There's a volunteer list over there behind the door." He grabbed the list from the wall. "You have to try and find a volunteer willing to come in. I only make a few phone calls, and then I give up. The four o'clock volunteer can pick up the slack."

I sat there thinking about how the shelter sometimes had difficulty getting a volunteer to come in from midnight to four in the morning. I remember once, when I came in at 4:00 a.m. to volunteer, the 12 to 4 volunteer didn't show up. The place was a mess. The clients' laundry wasn't done, the lunches weren't made, and there wasn't anything set up for the clients' breakfast. I couldn't just let some volunteer come walking into that. I got out of my seat and said, "Hey, I'm going to the back to see what's up."

As I walked out of the office, I heard Chicken Nugget say, "I don't think you should be doing that. That's a volunteer's job!"

I walked into the laundry room and noticed about 12 bags of client laundry. The laundry room had two huge front-load washers and two dryers. There was always plenty of laundry soap in the cabinets and even downstairs in the basement. I started to do the wash. We no longer had to fold laundry for clients. When laundry was done, we just had to set it in the hallway in a clean laundry basket until the client asked for it. For the wash, all you had to do was write down the client's name and time on this document, place the client's laundry bag on top of the washer it went into, and transfer it to the dryer later.

As I walked toward the office, I knew I wouldn't get into any trouble because all I was doing was helping out, which Al and Dick paid me to do. I wanted to help out. Chicken Nugget seemed very upset when I came into the office. He said, "What in the hell do you think you're doing? I'm the boss of this shift. I'm training you! You got it? Don't think you know how to run the place because you slept on the floor here. If we start to do the work back there every time a volunteer doesn't show up, they will expect us to do it all the time! I'm just happy, sitting here surfing on the web all night."

I glanced down at him sitting in the chair. He wasn't going to bully me. There was only one time in my childhood that I was bullied. It was the first day at Milltown Grade School when I started kindergarten. I got into a fight with two other kindergartens and lost the fight. It's never easy fighting two people at once. I went home that day and never said anything to my parents about the fight, but I did tell my brother Chum.

My brother Chum was one year younger, so he couldn't go to school yet, but I had him meet me at school the next day. The school was only one block from my parent's house, and back in those days, a child was safe to walk the streets. We met up with those two boys who beat me up, and my brother and I beat them up. That was the start of a long week for the James boys.

Well, one of the kindergarteners had an older brother. He brought his older brother, a sixth grader, to find me and my brother after school the next day. Well, sorry to say, those two boys also got beaten up that day. The following day after school, my brother and I had to fight a fifth-grader and a sixth-grader. We won that fight too. The day after, we were beating up some more sixth graders when Ms. Shoe, the kindergarten teacher, came and grabbed me by my ear and carted me off to the principal's office. My brother Chum followed behind us.

Ms. Shoe and the principal sent a note home with me and my brother Chum that day. I was only in kindergarten and couldn't read at the time. A few years later, my brother Chum and I found out what that note said: "Mr. and Mrs. James, could you please not have Jimmy have his young brother Chum follow him to school or meet him after school? We are asking because they are fighting with sixth graders and beating them up, which is embarrassing not just for the sixth graders but also for the school. We are requesting a meeting at your earliest convenience."

My father never did punish me or my brother for the fights that week. I think he was kind of happy that his boys were backing each other up when they needed help. My mother still has the note in her attic to this date.

"Did you have any luck contracting a volunteer to come in?" I asked. I counted the names listed on the worker's list. "Well, it looks like we need eight lunches for in the morning."

He placed the phone back on the charger and then answered, "No, no one answered any of the calls." He continued, "Hey, Jimmy, you need to sit down for a minute so we can have a talk here. I like you and all, but if you're not going to listen to me, I'll have no choice but to tell Dick and Al that you're not listening to me, and you don't want to be trained."

"There was nothing to talk about. The shelter needed my help. The workers needed lunches for in the morning, and the clients needed their laundry done. If Dick and Al were going to fire me for helping out, then I really don't want to work here then. I made all the lunches and even set up the breakfast cart for the clients' morning breakfast. I even kept all the washers and dryers going. There I was, doing the clients' laundry and making lunches. I used to come in and volunteer to do it, and now, I was getting paid to do it.

"It took me all night to do everything, but when the four o'clock volunteer showed up, everything was all set up for them. Chicken Nugget wasn't happy with me and didn't do any of the wake-up calls. I did them all. He even got into an argument with some of the clients over lunches again. I just didn't know why he had a problem handing out lunches to the working clients. It didn't come out of his pocket if a working client received a lunch."

Later that afternoon, Al called me. I couldn't believe it; Chicken Nugget had called Dick and Al on me."

I told Al I didn't do anything wrong by going to the back and helping out. I said, "The volunteer didn't show up, and what's his problem handing out lunches to working clients?"

Al agreed with me. He said, "Dick and I like how you took the initiative and have become a mentor at the shelter. You just keep on doing what you are doing. Dick and I hired two more people today. Hey, do you remember a staff person who worked here for about a month when you were sleeping on the floor? His name is Han."

"Yeah, I remember talking with Han a few times." Han was a very intelligent, highly neurotic computer "geek," an information service professional, to be precise. He graduated from the fine private college, Wood University in Wood County, Wisconsin, with a degree in computer science. Unfortunately, the rigors of the field led him to drink heavily. He became an alcohol abuser, eventually crashed from the juice, and ended up in rehab. Of course, now he lounges on the pink clouds of recovery and manifests his real character through a lingering dry drunk.

I asked, "Isn't that the person Raine fired for not getting along with clients?"

"There are a lot of changes coming to the shelter," he said, "Stuff I can't tell you about right now, Jimmy. On Wednesday, you'll be training a new person. Her name is Susan."

That night, I worked with Stephanie. The 12 to 4 volunteer didn't show up again. I went in back and did all the work that needed to be done; however, it didn't take me as long. When I was done with all the work in the back, I went on Craigslist to look for employment for the employment book. Stephanie told me how she and Chicken Nugget went at it the other night when they worked together. I guess whenever they worked together, they would irritate each other so badly that they wouldn't even talk to each other the whole shift. She also told me that she and Bobbie would take over the shelter. She showed me the monthly schedule she made. She also mentioned that I had nothing to worry about because they would keep me on the overnight shifts, five nights straight with no weekends. Stephanie and Bobbie thought that because they were hiring more people, Al and Thrifty would be fired for sure, and they would take over the shelter. They planned to have Bella do service point.

That morning, I placed the client employment book on the breakfast table where the clients were eating. I made my rounds, asking clients who didn't have food share to go down and sign up. There was only a handful of clients who didn't have food share. They all said they would sign up.

I knew the office door would be closed all night the following evening at work. It was so easy to make Rubio laugh. Whenever we had a few beers together, I just made her laugh all night. I walked into the office and saw her face. She wasn't happy at all. After I showed her how to do a physical head count and check the client log-in book, the count was on, and Bobbie and Bella left for the night. She couldn't believe how many clients were sleeping on the floor. It was a sad thing to see, especially the women sleeping on the floor.

I said, "The numbers just keep going up. When Raine oversaw the shelter, the numbers would reach around 35, maybe 40. Now the numbers are up to 45 to 50 a night."

She had this sad look on her face and responded, "There's really nine women sleeping out there on those little green mats."

I bit down on my bottom lip and nodded my head up and down, pulling a white envelope out of my back pocket. "Check this out! I got it today in the mail." I handed her the letter I got from the Department of Workforce Development Equal Rights Division, which read:

> Dear Mr. James, we have received your wage complaint and have sent the enclosed Notice of Complaint to the employer you named. The notice requires the employer to respond to me within two weeks. Due to the large caseload, the resolution of complaints is taking longer than normal. It is not uncommon for these investigations to take several months, depending on the workload. We ask for your patience during the investigation. We understand that you may not be willing or able to await the resolution of your case at this level. All wage complaints may be filed either with this division or in Circuit Court (Small Claims Court) if the amount at issue is less than $10,000. Notify me if you decide to instead pursue the claim in court or if your claim has been settled so that we may close our file on this matter.
>
> Dear Employer: A complaint has been filed under Wisconsin Statute 109.09, Wisconsin's Wage Payment and Collection Law, by Mr. Jimmy James, who claims you

are indebted to him for mileage. A copy of the complaint is enclosed.

The Department is obligated under this statute to gather and review the facts involved in this complaint. If you believe the complaint is incorrect, please submit your position in writing along with any documentation that might disprove the complaint and support your position.

If you agree that the complaint is valid and wish to resolve this matter, I request you forward a check made out to the complaint for the claims wages, less standard deductions. You must also include a check stub or a similar statement showing the amount of and reason for each deduction from wages. Payment should be sent to my attention, but the check must be made payable to the complaint. In either case, an answer is required in writing.

When Rubio was done reading the document, I handed her the next envelope from the Department of Workforce Development Equal Rights Division, which read:

Dear Ms. Jackson: Per our telephone conversation, please find enclosed a check in the amount of $12.60, payable to Jimmy James. This payment is to reimburse Mr. James for mileage expenses.

As we had discussed, I would like to state that this payment does not in any way admit guilt on the part of Wood County Packaging but was much simpler and easier than preparing a rebuttal to his complaint. I am assuming that once this payment is made, this case will be closed. Thanking you for your help in settling this complaint.

Enclosed is a check along with a reply from Wood County Packaging in response to the above-referenced wage claim. With the payment of this check, you have been paid in full. Therefore, I am closing your case file at this time. Please contact me if you have any questions concerning this matter.

I held up the check to show her. "I can't wait until next Friday before the unemployment judge. I'll be getting my money that day, too."

She agreed that I would win hands down. The rest of the night, we talked about Tia and how she was doing since the intervention. I guess she was doing better, but Rubio still had to be on her toes with Tia. She even told Al straight up that this would be the only overnight shift she could work because she wanted to be home to keep an eye on Tia.

Rubio asked me occasionally how it was being locked up in prison. I told her the story about when I was driving for the prison system, making a dollar an hour. Yeah, I was laying up in the infirmary for about two months, healing from the gunshot wounds, when they transferred me to Walker's Prison. It was a minimum security prison. I only had 15 more months to do, and I had a driver's license, which was like having a free pass to get out of prison each day. I was like a trustee. The guard would give me the keys to one of their vans, and I would be responsible for driving convicts to certain locations so they could go to work.

One day, I picked up four convicts. One was Pedro, who had a dark blue five-star tattoo on the back of his neck. He was from Chicago and a high-ranking Tri-City Bomber.

Then, there was Thomas, whom Pedro looked out for in prison. He was just a young kid, maybe 23 years old and maybe 120 pounds. He was going home in four months to his wife and three children. They both got into the back seat of the 1998 Dodge Caravan.

Big Mike was another convict. He was an African American, at least 6'7 and 350 pounds. He was the biggest person in the prison. He had a hard time getting into the sliding side door of the van, so he had to sit sideways on the bench seat. The last person was Fred, who jumped up front in the passenger front seat by me and lit up a smoke. He was around a 35-year-old White boy. He didn't even have a felony charge; he was sent to prison for just two years. The judge in his county got sick and tired of him with his 25 misdemeanors.

Here we were, rolling down Highway 43, doing about 70mph, when I looked in the rear-view mirror and saw Pedro with this nickel ninety-five smile on his face. He was about to do something he was thinking about all day at work. I really didn't know what it was all about until I was called into the Capitan's office when I got back to prison with five police officers present. It was all over some women at work. Big Mike was trying to move in on Pedro's main squeeze at work. I guess they were having sex at work, and Big Mike wanted some of the action. Pedro went off big time on Big Mike. He leaned forward and started to throw rights and lefts into Big Mike's face. Big Mike was trying to fight back, but his right arm was pinned up against the back seat. He threw a couple of lefts, but they really didn't have any effect.

I pulled over on the closest ramp, got out, lit up a cigarette, and watched the fight from outside through the front windshield. Fred also got out of the vehicle as we both watched the fight and saw how Thomas managed to make it out of the back seat without getting kicked or punched as he opened up the sliding side door of the van.

As the two were fighting, I noticed a bunch of cars getting off the highway and passing us. One car stopped, and a woman came running up to me, asking me, "Why aren't you doing anything?"

She thought because I was dressed in blue jeans and a gray shirt that, I was a prison guard driving the convicts around.

"Lady, I'm going home in two months," I said. "You better stay away from that van because those boys aren't playing."

She headed toward the van and, on her way there, she called for backup, saying, "Off-duty police officer needs assistance."

There were four police cars there within seconds. Big Mike and Pedro were handcuffed and carted off to a maximum prison that day. I guess the lady at the work site was fired.

⟡ ⟡ ⟡ ⟡

The following night, I had to train Susan. Susan had long black hair and brown eyes. She stood 5'7" and was a little thick, around 175 pounds. She was taking computer classes online in the Human Health Field. She was divorced with a little boy around 15 years old.

I gave Susan the following instructions:

I want you to document everything we do tonight. That way, it will be written up, and everybody will know what needs to be done and when. The 11:00 person must check to make sure lunches are made. If lunches are not made, the 8 to 12 volunteer will make them.

At 11:15, do a check on the chores list to make sure all chores are signed up for in the morning. The chores list has three days. Make a list of names and check the spreadsheet to see if the client has been staying at the shelter for the last three days. If a client has been staying for three days and has not done a chore, assign them a chore in the morning by signing their name and notifying them of why they have been assigned the chore.

At 11:30, remove all dirty towels in the laundry baskets in all the clients' bathrooms and replace them with clean, empty laundry baskets. At 12:00, verify the headcount and keep the clients' wash going until done. Place the clean laundry by the office on the check-in table. Place clean towels in the women's and handicapped bathrooms. Men's clean towels go into the office closet. Any bedding that is washed on the shift should be placed in intake bins and set out by the office. If no bins are needed, place all the bedding in the proper cabinets. Never start laundry after 6:45 a.m. because it can't stay in the washing machine until 5:00 p.m. the next day. If there is a new intake to be done, the lead person will be responsible for doing it unless the staff member wants to do it. Follow the same procedure as the night shift for new intakes.

At 12:30, check the coffee cart to make sure coffee is made for nonworking clients and that there are coffee cups on the cart. Make sure there's enough sugar, creamer, and stir sticks on the cart. Set up the coffee pot on the counter for working clients. Start the coffee about 10 minutes before the first wake-up call.

At 12:45, set up the cereal cart and place the four cereal containers on the cart, along with spoons, cups, oatmeal, cereal bowls, and four silver trays. Never dump new cereal on top of old cereal in cereal containers, and never mix two different types of cereal into a cereal container.

At 1:00, twice weekly, do a check for wants and warrants on clients. On Wednesdays, do a worker's verification. Go back seven days on the workers' sign-in sheet and make a list of clients' names. Grab the worker's verification folder from the non-active filing cabinet, review the names, and make a list of clients not handing in proper employment records. Place the clients' names on the chalkboard and the number of weeks the client is behind, showing proper documentation that they are working.

Also, pull out bread for breakfast and lunches for the next day. Ensure there is enough lunch meat in the refrigerator for lunches the following day; if not, pull some out from the freezer. Fill the sink with hot, soapy water for dishes to soak so that when the 5 to 8 volunteer comes in, they can easily handle them. Check on hard-boiled eggs. On average, clients go through 2-3 dozen eggs daily for breakfast.

At 1:30, empty all the trash from all the bathrooms and check for contraband. Empty the office trash, take out the garbage from the kitchen, and empty the recycle bin in the kitchen. Put out all cleaning supplies for the clients to do chores in the morning.

Ten minutes before the first wake-up call, set out the food cart for working clients with coffee, coffee cups, cups, juice, sugar, creamer, bowls, hard-boiled eggs, cereal, salt, and pepper. A working client is responsible for picking up their mat and bin. Start handing out lunches to working clients. If a client is leaving the shelter and has a weapon locked up in the lockers, the client has to step out into the locked lobby. The lead person will go into the locker, grab the weapon, and hand it to the client through the security tray.

At 4:00, greet the volunteer at the door and ask them if they have been to the shelter before. Show them how to sign in and the dry good cart going out for breakfast. At 5:55, explain to the volunteer that all the items will be placed on the counter for the clients for breakfast. Turn on the sanitizer and show the volunteer the laundry room. If it's their first time, you might have to help serve breakfast. If a volunteer does not show up, check the calendar behind the office door and call in a volunteer. Make a note of this in the shift report.

At 5:55, turn on the canister lights, bring out the non-working coffee cart, and plug it in. At 6:00, serve breakfast and unlock the smoke door. Turn on both TVs. One TV goes on the Weather Channel, and the other on the news channel. At 6:30, turn on all lights and wake up any remaining clients. A client may need to use the bathroom, get something to eat, put their bedding away, and maybe even smoke a cigarette before they even think about doing a chore.

The staff driver will show up at 6:30, read the previous shift report, and look at any new intakes. The driver will retrieve the keys from the office closet and greet the volunteer, asking if they require any assistance. At 6:45, check on the chores list and make sure clients are doing chores. At 7:00, talk with the driver and start van rides. The driver must walk around the van to do a safety check before entering the van. Also, the driver must fill out the driver's logbook in the van with the date, miles, and destination. Shut down the breakfast cart and coffee cart at 7:00. The 11 to 7 staff member will thank the volunteer for their help and then leave.

At 7:45, check to ensure no clients are outside smoking before locking the smoke door. At 7:50, remove all dirty towels from all the clients' bathrooms and replace them with clean, empty laundry baskets. Refill any personal hygiene items in all the clients' bathrooms. Thank the volunteer for coming in.

At 8:00, lock up the active filing cabinet, turn off the monitor for the security camera, send off the shift report, turn off the monitor for the computer, and transfer the phone over. Do a walk-through to ensure no clients are in the building and all windows are closed and locked before leaving for the morning. Also, make sure the entrance door is locked.

I sent Al and Dick an email with the document Susan and I had worked on the night before. It was a guideline of what needed to be done on the overnight shift in case a volunteer didn't show up. I also suggested possibly getting rid of the 12 to 4 volunteer and moving the hours to 5:00 – 8:00 in the morning for two reasons. The first reason is that I noticed it's a hard spot to keep filled, and the second is the staff needs something to do at night.

The following night, I had to work with Han. I already knew what he was thinking—how he was so much better than me because he went to college, and I used to sleep on the floor as a homeless client. As we sat in the office, you could feel the tension in the air. Finally, I heard, "You know, Dick hired me back because he didn't think I was too hard on the clients last time I worked here. You, of all people, should know how that goes when people have drug and alcohol problems. Dick told me, when he hired me back that he wants me to push the clients to stop using."

I contemplated the brief comment regarding drug and alcohol use. I was unsure whether it was intended positively or negatively towards me. However, one thing was certain: he would have a hard time when working with clients dealing with drug and alcohol problems. One thing I learned when I slept on the floor is when a staff member would leave the shelter, their name would echo throughout the walls for months. Han's name echoed in the shelter in a bad way.

He grabbed the phone and remarked, "We don't have a volunteer for the night yet. I'm going to make a few phone calls to see if I can find a volunteer to come in for the shift."

"Well, I guess I'll go in back and see what's up back there," I said, getting out of my chair and checking the document to see how many working clients' lunches needed to be made. "It looks like we need nine lunches made up for the morning," I alerted him as I walked out of the office and headed for the kitchen.

Both washers and dryers were done. I got them all going again. After I was done with that, I started making lunches. Han came marching into the kitchen, saying, "Hey, we need to talk. I'm in charge here, not you, and I don't think you should be back here doing a volunteer's job when 49 clients are sleeping on the floor out there. Now, I want you to put all of this stuff away and come back to the office. I don't think you get the whole picture here. What would happen if an intake shows up?"

I wasn't going to put anything back until I was done making lunches. If an intake did show up, they had to fill out all the paperwork before they could enter. I didn't care what he thought. I knew he wasn't my boss. Al and Dick were my bosses, and they didn't mind me being back there helping out when a volunteer didn't show up. When I was done setting everything up, I went out the back door to smoke. I stayed off camera so Han couldn't watch me on the monitor. After, I walked back into the office and sat down. I already knew Han would go off on me, but I wasn't a client anymore. I was a staff member, just like he was.

"Why didn't you listen to me when I told you to put everything away and come back to the office?" He said, as he let out a sigh.

"Hey, let me sit over there so I can check my email and show you why I did what I did."

We traded office chairs, so I would be in front of the computer. He continued to go on and on, "I don't know what you think you are going to show me on the computer; that's going to change my mind. I told you earlier tonight that I'm in charge and will run the place the same way I did last time I worked here."

I was about to show him the email from Dick and Al, saying they wanted me to help out in the back when a volunteer didn't show up, but then I saw an e-mail from Debbie. It read:

"I think it's a great idea that you have to move the midnight to 4:00 a.m. volunteer hours to 5:00 to 8:00 in the morning. It is a hard slot to fill. I agree staff can pick up the slack until the volunteer shows up. I have to get permission from the board before we can move forward with your idea. Keep up the good work at the shelter."

I said, "Come read the email." You should've seen his face when he was done reading it. I then clicked on the email I sent to Dick and Al about Susan and me setting up step-by-step how the overnight shift should operate.

Their email read, "Susan called them this morning and said she really liked working with you last night and how you showed her the overnight shift step-by-step. We're going to be hiring more staff. At least we have something set up for them to go on now."

You should've really seen his face then. He didn't know what to say. After that, I showed him the document Susan and I submitted to Dick and Al. Then I said, "This is how the overnight shift is going to be run. I will be working this shift four nights a week, and you work it two nights a week."

I also showed him the F-Set Program I had set up.

Later that morning, when all the clients were up, I went around asking the clients who didn't have food share if they went down to sign up. A few clients got annoyed by me asking the same question every morning. One asked, "When will you stop sweating me over food share?"

I told the client straight out, "When you go down and sign up and show me the food share card."

Many clients began sharing their thoughts on my role in running the shelter. Some were pleased to have one of their peers working there, remarking, "At least you understand what we're experiencing."

One even remarked, "The man who gave up the Tri-City Bomber gang to become a leader of a homeless shelter."

I was becoming a big-time leader at the shelter. It felt like I was back in the gang again; just this time, I was the leader, a shot caller. Clients would come up to me with different questions and ask for different kinds of advice. I had an answer for everything. I was in a zone. I finally found the job I was training for my whole life, and I didn't even know it at the time. I basically lived it all.

As I started to think about the night back in 1978, that was one crazy night. One of my vatos gave me a key to a hotel room. He was done using the room. He only rented the room because he had some customers coming from out of town to do drug deals. I grabbed the key from him. Why not? All the drug deals were done with. I called my girlfriend, Donna, to see if she wanted to kick it at a hotel for the night. I went out and got a few bottles of wine for us. Donna and I were going out for about 18 months at the time.

I don't have to get into any details about what Donna and I did that night. Suddenly, we both heard someone trying to open the door. I jumped out of bed as quickly as I could and just in the nick of time. They already had the door cracked open when I slammed into it to close it shut. Donna grabbed her clothes, headed into the bathroom, and locked the door behind her. I didn't know what to think. Was it a bad drug deal, and the people came back to get revenge? There was a struggle over the door for a few minutes. I even heard, "Milltown Police Department." I didn't believe it, not for one minute. I thought they were lying so that I would open the door.

Well, only seconds later, the Milltown Police Department was in the hotel room. The "po-po" just came bashing through the door. The hotel manager and his kid were the first set of people who tried to enter the hotel room that night. The kid saw a lot of other people coming and going all day from the hotel room and told his father about it. When his father found time, he came to investigate what was happening in the room.

The "po-po" allowed me to get dressed before they arrested me that day. The first count was carrying a concealed weapon. I had a 6" switchblade knife in my front pocket; it was just a misdemeanor, and I ended up paying a $189.00 fine. The second charge was criminal trespassing; it also was a misdemeanor because I didn't pay for the room. For that one, I had to pay for the room and a fine of $220.00.

The third charge was a little bit more serious. I was charged with statutory rape. Donna was only 17 years old, and I was 18. Needless to say, our parents didn't agree with that charge one bit. We met with the District Attorney and then in front of the judge. The deal was that Donna and I would have one more weekend together before she would commit to a 30-day alcohol program. I also had to pay a fine for contributing to a minor, which amounted to $262.00. Before we got to the hotel, I picked up a few bottles of wine to get us in the mood. I was charged with statutory rape. I paid the court costs and a fine of $450.00.

The following night, I had to work with Klazina. She told me about the conversation with Dick and Al earlier that day about Chicken Nugget.

"They fired him today," she said, with a smile on her face. "It's about time. He didn't have a clue on how to treat clients around here, not at all. They also mentioned you, Jimmy, and how the clients respect you and everything you're doing here at the shelter, like getting clients to sign up for food share and finding employment."

I said, "Yeah, every time a client signs for food share, F-Set Program, or found employment, I type it up in the shift notes. I've been in management before, so I know someone higher up reads the shift reports and would want to know the progress of the clients. Why wouldn't they want to know?"

Klazina said, "I don't know if anyone told you yet, but Al is leaving the shelter. He put his two weeks' notice in today. He is going to work in the prison system as an A.O.D.A. counselor. I think they're going to make me the next case manager of the shelter."

My mouth opened wide like I was trying to catch flies. Klazina must've noticed it because she said, "Oh, you don't have anything to worry about when I become the next case manager; I'm going to keep you. I will make you lead on the overnight shifts with no weekends."

It was nice that Klazina said she would make me the lead on the overnight shift, but I really didn't think they would make her a case manager of the shelter unless they knew something about her that I didn't know. I sat there watching the clients sleep. I'd been in management before, so I knew people got their walking papers when a new boss came into play.

As I started to run down the list of employees at the shelter, Bobbie and Stephanie agreed that I would go to the overnight shift as lead. Klazina also said the same thing.

Bella said she would start doing service point. Rubio and Susan just started working at the shelter, and Thrifty was out of the picture. They had cut his hours for starting things in the office and not wanting to do service point. Han was the only other person left, and there was no way they would make him a case manager. He didn't get along with the clients or staff, and if they did make him case manager, he wouldn't last long.

I was all good. I had nothing to worry about. A few seconds passed, and I thought about the e-mail I showed Han a few nights ago. They were hiring more staff. I sat there for a minute or two. I had nothing to worry about. All I had to do was keep doing what I was doing: helping clients.

The following night, before Al and I started to check clients into the shelter, I asked about him leaving the shelter. I said, "Hey, I heard a rumor that you are leaving the shelter to work in the prison system. Is that true?"

As he unlocked the door so the clients could enter, he said, "I'm done here! I had enough of it." He pointed his finger toward the office where Thrifty and Bobbie were. "It's impossible working with them two, and I'm not even going to get into about the other staff working here. Everybody here thinks my job is so easy. Well, good luck with that when I'm gone. Sometime later tonight, Jimmy, you need to get with Thrifty and get that service point stuff worked out."

Later that night, I walked into the office. It was the first time I had heard Thrifty and Bobbie talking to each other. Bobbie finally got up and walked out of the office. That's when I noticed Thrifty placing something in Klazina's mailbox. After that, he sat down to send an email to service point, explaining what happened with the leak. He already had it all typed up. The message included that I had walked in on him while he was doing service point. It wasn't the truth, but it wasn't a big deal to me if he wanted to lie to them.

He clicked send and said, "You better hope I never catch you drinking on the job. Han told me all about it, how you went off of all of the cameras and then came back in smelling like alcohol."

I looked over at him. If looks could kill, he would've been dead. I angrily said, "What are you talking about? I wasn't drinking on the job. You have things mixed up, like always, just like service point. When I had my bi-weekly meeting with Judy, she asked me how I was doing down here. I told her that the intake process made sense to me after you showed me how to do service point."

As he started to walk out of the office, he said, "You can't be homeless and working at a homeless shelter. I'm going to have to talk to someone about this."

That weekend, I was off, but Rubio had to work, and she started to text me all these crazy texts. I guess she and Susan didn't get along with Bobbie. Bobbie was telling the two how she would be the boss of the Shelter. The following night wasn't much better for Rubio. She told me that Han and Stephanie went at it in front of all the clients and that she didn't like working with either. I guess even Susan texted Rubio later that night when she was working with Bella to complain about how she was being treated.

Rubio later texted, "Susan and I think you should be in charge of the shelter. You know how to treat people."

I sat there thinking about the text. I knew I could do the job and would be good at it, too. I mean, I had been living it for three years, and some of the clients were my friends from when I lived on the floor with them, and they did respect me.

I was starting to set things up at the shelter, but there was no way I would get the job. How would that look? The new case manager of the shelter is living at Project Homes. That would be something the Italian mob crime bosses or gang leaders would do when they were incarcerated in prison. They still called the shots for their outfits on the streets. The board members would never go for something like that.

The following work week was just crazy. The cliques formed. Al tried his best to control everything that was going on in the office, but it was out of hand. Dick and Al hired three more people to start work the following week. It seemed like Bobbie and Stephanie had taken over already. They didn't like Han, Thrifty, Klazina, Rubio or Susan. They were going to keep Bella to do service point and me on the overnights.

Klazina thought she would be in charge and was running around hanging up all these instructions on what a client could and couldn't do, but the funny thing is she never took down the old postings. She would just put the new posting next to the old posting, even if the instructions had changed. She was keeping me, and either Rubio or Susan would do service point. Bella played both sides of the fence. She teamed up with Bobbie and Stephanie, but when she worked with Thrifty, it was a different story. Thrifty was going to give her service point if he became the boss. Thrifty was keeping Rubio, Susan, and Han. I heard from Rubio that Thrifty said I wasn't a keeper.

❖❖❖❖❖

It was Friday. I heard the administrative law judge for unemployment call the case. I looked around but didn't see anyone from Wood County Packaging in the courtroom. I heard the case being called again. I sat in the brown leather office chair and unfolded the paper with my questions for Wood County Packaging.

The judge sat up high behind the shiny cherry bench. She was an older woman, maybe in her late sixties, with short gray hair. "Mr. James, I'll be with you in just a few minutes. I'm going to try to make contact with the defendant." Jill from the Human Resources Department answered the phone. The judge asked, "Is there some reason why you're not in the courtroom today?"

The judge had her on speaker, so I could hear everything she was saying. She said, "I contacted someone in your office a few days ago, saying that we wouldn't be able to make the meeting and would have to do it online."

I just sat tight. How unprofessional was this? I wasn't buying it, and the judge wasn't either. The judge asked, "Could you please give me the name of the person you contacted in my office so that I could verify this?"

It was getting better and better as it went on. She answered, "No, I don't recall the person's name off hand."

The judge was mixed with African American and Spanish. She made a few adjustments and then went online. "Okay, do you see me?" she asked Jill.

"Yes, and I just want to mention that Steve just entered my office and will be sitting in on the hearing today."

The judge looked at the monitor and said, "Could you please be seated in front of the monitor, sir, and tell me your job title?"

"I'm the safety manager of Wood County Packaging."

After the judge swore us in and stated the case with all the facts from both parties, she asked Jill and Steve if there were any questions that they wanted to ask her.

I swear to God, I couldn't believe what came out of Steve's mouth. This had to have been his first time ever at an unemployment hearing. He said, "You mean we can ask questions?"

I laughed deep down inside and wondered where in the hell they got that guy from.

Jill started, "Well, when I did my investigation with Eric, I learned two things. The first thing Eric said was that you wanted to get fired, and you exhibited disruptive behavior. Secondly, the clients felt fearful for a few days before your termination."

The judge stared down at me as she used her right index finger to slide her black-framed glasses up her nose. "Well, Mr. James, did you want to quit your job?"

I shook my head back and forth and answered, "No, I didn't want to quit my job, and for that last comment, if the clients feared for their lives, do they have any witnesses to prove this?"

Steve spoke up loudly. "Yes, I do. From my investigation, Eric told me that you wanted to get fired and were disruptive when you worked around the clients."

The judge interrupted Steve. "Let me ask you, why isn't Eric here testifying?"

I sat there picturing Eric on the production floor the day he fired me, just screaming at the top of his lungs, "I'm going to fight your unemployment all the way."

"Yeah, where was Eric, that little mental midget?"

Steve answered, "Oh, because I was the one who did the investigation. I didn't think we needed all these people."

"Is there anything else, sir?" The judge asked.

Jill interjected, "My next question is concerning a phone call I had with him. Did I ever use the word termination during the phone call?"

I thought, *What kind of question is this?* I answered, "I'm not really sure what words you used that day—my services weren't required; I was fired or terminated—but I was no longer going to be employed by Wood County Packaging. That's what I got out of the conversation."

"Is there anything else you wish to ask Mr. James at this time?" The judge asked.

That was all they had. It was finally my turn to ask some questions. I only had a few questions I thought the judge would like to hear. I said, "Your handbook states the following protocol should take place with an employee before the employee can be fired. Could you please explain today why the verbal warning, the written warning, or the three-day suspension never took place? Why did it go to the final warning, and why didn't you follow your own protocol?"

"Well, as Steve said before, he investigated the situation and found that you were very disruptive around the clients; that's why it went straight to the final warning."

This was enough of the same story! I had to shut this down. "This is only hearsay; they don't even have a witness to testify to this, your Honor."

Right after that, I asked, "You say that I wanted to get fired from Wood County Packaging so I could collect unemployment; is that correct?"

They both couldn't get the words out fast enough. "Yeah, yes."

"Well, your Honor, I'm a little lost on this one because two weeks to the date after I was fired from Wood County Packaging, I started working at the shelter as a Night Safety Manager, making $2.00 more an hour. Your Honor, I have a few pay stubs with the date on them."

They tried to ask a few more questions, but even the judge thought they were reaching and called the case. She said, "I will have a decision within two to four weeks."

Within a few days, I received the notice stating I won my unemployment case and the funds would be direct deposited into my bank account.

At my next bi-weekly goal meeting with Judy, my goals were to save money from my unemployment for housing, save more money out of my paycheck, continue progress on my next book, and maintain stable employment.

Down at the shelter, all hell broke loss. Stephanie was gone, and Bobbie put in her two weeks' notice. I guess the two of them set up this meeting with some board members about Al, and the outcome wasn't good for either. Even Al had enough of it. He was done working at the shelter, even though he only had one more day before he started his new job. Klazina also put her two weeks' notice in.

Thrifty became the new manager. It was crazy! He started trouble right off the bat. Bobbie only lasted two days with him, and she was gone. He didn't play any games with her. She just wasn't going to work for him. Thrifty wasn't as nice to Klazina as he was to Bobbie. Klazina found all kinds of strange things in her mailbox. Even when she would go down into the basement to keep it organized, Thrifty would make fun of her in front of all the staff as they watched her on the cameras, saying, "Does she even know what she's doing down there?"

Klazina took care of the basement ever since she started at the shelter, and I thought she did a good job down there. The basement had just about anything you imagined a homeless person would need. Thrifty let it be known to me personally that I only had a few weeks after Klazina was gone before I was fired. He also said they just hired more people, and when they were trained, I would be fired. However, I had different plans. He was just a game player with a title, which didn't mean anything to me. I knew I was smarter than him, without a doubt.

The people Dick and Al hired started to show up to work. One was a cute little thing named Karla. She was maybe 22, around 5'5", with a slim 115-pound body. She had two children already and was on this program set up by Wood County, where daycare would be free if you volunteered or worked at a nonprofit organization. Not only were clients infatuated with Karla, but Thrifty was Thrifty when it came to her. She was almost wearing nothing for clothes and would wittingly turn on the charm when talking to him. Like a dirty old man, he fell for everything: hook, line, and sinker.

Thrifty never had a chance with her, but in his dirty little mind, he thought he did because he was the boss of the shelter. It was kind of funny he had Bobbie go down and talk to Donald about Al hitting on women clients, but he was doing the same thing, just that it was with working staff. He gave Bella the password to do service point when he became the manager, but it was a different story when Karla showed up. He gave her the password and told her she could bank her hours from home when she did service point.

Once Bella found out what Thrifty did with service point, she left the job and never returned. I already knew they were going to have problems on that shift. You had four good-looking women on the shift, with Han and Thrifty in the middle of all of it. The cliques formed right away. One consisted of Rubio and Susan, both of whom felt they should have been approached to take on service points. The other clique included Karla and her friend Jazmine. According to what I heard from other clients, Jazmine and Karla had initially met at a nonprofit organization with free daycare about a year ago.

Jazmine was an African American woman around 23 years old. She had three children, but you couldn't tell by looking at her. She was very cute and intelligent. She noticed right away that Thrifty had no leadership skills. She actually started planning how to take Thrifty's job. Interestingly, none of the ladies got along with Han. The only person who got along with him was Thrifty. The reason was because Han knew a lot about the computer system.

Thrifty scheduled me to work five overnight shifts straight from Monday to Friday. He took me off the only night shift I had. When I asked him about it, he said there's a lot of new staff, and he would be busy training them all. I knew what it was all about; he didn't want me to be around the clients because the clients looked up to me, and I would want to help them out on the night shifts. Well, I was stuck on the overnight shift.

It was Jordy's first night at the shelter. Jordy was a big boy who stood at least 6'7" and around 300 pounds. He made me look like a midget standing next to him. He was inked up and had a shiny, clean bald head. I told him my story, and then he told me his. He was born and raised in Wood County. When he graduated from high school, his father got him a job working with him at Wood County Paper. His father worked there for his entire life. He was married for 13 years and had no children. He had a disagreement with management about working on Sundays at his last job. That was his wife's only day off, and he wanted to spend time with her. That's how he ended up working at the shelter. When Dick and Al hired him, they both reassured him that he wouldn't have to work on Sundays.

Jordy wanted to learn and wasn't afraid to help out. He wasn't like the old staff who just wanted to sit in the office all night; he wanted to help in the back. I printed up the checklist that Susan and I made. After that, we went to the back, and I showed him the kitchen and laundry room. I explained everything to him and asked if he had any questions. I told him they used to have a volunteer from 12 to 4, but it was too hard to fill that slot, so staff now sets everything up until the five o'clock volunteer shows up. I helped him out a little bit, but he had it already.

After we were all set up in the back, I showed him the F-Set Program. A few more clients went down and signed up for food share. All the clients staying at the shelter now had food share. I showed him the shift report and typed up the clients' names who had signed up. I didn't think I was doing anything wrong; however, Thrifty sent me an email on the subject the next day.

He said, "Jimmy, please do not be putting in the shift notes about clients getting food share. The board members don't want to see this information. In addition, you have been putting in last names, which is inappropriate."

Thrifty had this saying at the end of his email. "'You must be the change you wish to see in the world.' Mahatma Gandhi." I was confused. I sent him back an email, asking, "Why wouldn't the board members want to know what was happening with the clients staying at the shelter and their last names? Why do we use a client's last name when they check into the shelter, then?"

He never replied to the email. I showed some of the staff in the office the email and said, "If they want to fire me for helping out clients, then they can go ahead and do it."

Thrifty never worked an overnight shift at the shelter. He had no clue what went down on the shift or who volunteered on the overnight shift. Well, Vice President Josh and his wife Betty would come in to volunteer every other Thursday morning. Josh told me to keep doing what I was doing and that they wanted to know the clients' progress.

A few days later, Thrifty made out the next two-week schedule. My days were changed. I had to work the next two weekends in a row. However, I wasn't the only one bitching about the schedule. Jordy was scheduled to work both Sundays. I guess that was our punishment for typing in the shift report about the clients getting food share.

Thrifty had also never worked a weekend either. In fact, I never worked a weekend, but I stayed a few weekends sleeping on the floor. The weekends weren't as busy. I knew I would have a lot of free time, so I set up the Social Security Disability Income (SSDI) Program. I clicked on a spreadsheet and went one by one through all the active client files. I typed in the client's name, the intake date, how much money they received monthly, and if they had a payee.

Seven clients were on SSDI. Out of the seven, two had been sleeping on the floor for over three months and making over $700.00 monthly. One of the clients even had a payee. I typed it up in the shift notes. Josh told me the board wanted to know what was happening with the clients, and someone had to start helping them. I had to work with Han a few nights later, and he told me that he and Thrifty discussed the programs I set up. They both agreed it would be too much work to run the programs. I thought for a second or two before I answered him. He and Thrifty were just jealous that I was setting things up and knew how to run the shelter. I told him straight out right to his face, "Well, anyone working at a shelter should be willing to go the extra mile to help a homeless client. I don't think it's too much work."

It would not be much work for anyone because the program was all set up. A client on SSDI would receive their checks on the 3rd of each month. This just had to be documented in the program, and the shelter would have a running total of how much the client had since they had been staying at the Shelter.

That morning, I asked a few clients on SSDI why they didn't have a payee. I heard a few different answers, such as, "A payee costs money each month, and when I need money, they won't give it to me. A payee won't allow me to buy what I want with my own money." That Sunday night, I checked to make sure all the lunches were made up for the working clients. The shelter now had 15 working clients. The employment book was working along with the F-Set program. Whenever I drove around town running errands and saw "help wanted" signs posted at companies, I would tell clients about those employment opportunities every morning.

CHAPTER THREE

HOUSING

I knew it wouldn't be easy to find a place to live. Ten landlords denied me before I found a landlord who would accept me. Judy at Project Homes allowed me to stay ten extra days past the program limit. It was like the Warming Shelter; they allowed me to stay a month and a half past the limit. It was almost a long four years that I was homeless. I left my efficiency apartment in Huntsville on September 7, 2010, and on August 10, 2014, I moved into my one-bedroom apartment. It was a big one-bed apartment. Tia and I loaded up the U-Haul truck and moved my furniture from my storage locker to my new place. I was all set up again: cable TV, Internet, and my bed and bathroom.

There was a program in Wood County for people who ran in hard times, where they would help you with rent and deposit money, but I didn't go that route. How would that look? I'm a night safety manager at a shelter begging for help. No way! I worked my way off of all government assistance, and I had money saved up. I even received a check from Judy for making my goals. I was sitting pretty good. Project Homes really did me justice.

The word of me finally finding my own place was big-time news at the shelter for a few weeks. All of the staff and the clients were happy for me, but not Thrifty. When the next two-week schedule came out, my hours were cut from 40 to 32 hours weekly. I was upset about this one. I went right over his head and called Dick. He knew I was getting my own place. Dick said not to worry about it and would talk to Thrifty about it to ensure I got my hours.

When I walked into the office that night, all the staff working that night were talking about it. I said, "If you take a second or two to think about it, he's a shelter manager, and he has a person working for him, fighting four years of homelessness, and he cut my hours when I finally found a place. Now we all know why the clients aren't moving and why we're at 50 every night. If he doesn't want me to make it, why would he want any of the clients sleeping on the floor to make it?"

Maxwell agreed with me. The shelter went through another hiring process. No one besides Han wanted to work for Thrifty. He thought because he was the boss that, people had to respect him, and that was it, but none of the staff saw it his way; we all thought he should be the one who showed more respect towards his staff. Maxwell had replaced Jordy on the overnight shifts. Jordy told Thrifty repeatedly that he couldn't work on Sundays, but Thrifty kept on scheduling him for Sundays. One Sunday, he just quit.

Maxwell and I were the same size. He was like Han, very smart with the computer system. He had shoulder-length brown hair and a mustache to match. He loved the kitchen at the shelter because he worked as a cook for years at Wood County Hotel. He was homeless for a year at one time in his life. His homelessness came from drug abuse while he attended college. He got hooked on Adderall while studying for exams and the late-night cramming sessions for tests. When he graduated from college, he was hooked on Adderall, and his connection was gone, so he turned to cocaine, which led to homelessness.

Maxwell was good with the clients, and the clients respected him. He and I came up with the client laundry checklist. I did the math in my head one day and concluded that 50 clients were staying at the shelter. That meant 100 loads of wash in a 7-day period, and there were two washers. It turned out to be seven loads between both washers.

As I checked the laundry list, I realized that something was going on. The laundry list only consisted of a client's name, the time the laundry went in, the time it went into the dryer, and the date it was done. I checked the names on the list. There it was! Some clients were doing their laundry every day. I wrote down all the clients' names who were misusing the laundry. I walked back into the office, grabbed a flashlight, and checked the clients' bins to see if they had clothes. I quickly shined the light on all the clients' bins, which were full of clothing.

I walked back into the office and told Maxwell what I just unearthed. We made up a document with the clients' names on one side and, on the top, the days of the week, Sunday through Saturday. There was a rule that a client could have their laundry done twice in a seven-day period.

Well, Thrifty was Thrifty on this one. He didn't want to change the rule. I tried to explain the difference between twice in a seven-day period and twice within a week. Thrifty said, "I'm not changing the rule. Staff and volunteers are just going to have to page back and forth to keep track of client's laundry."

Thrifty really showed staff how dumb he was on this one. All the staff agreed that the rule should've been changed. It was only common sense. Why would you want to have to page back and forth when you could just have it all on one page in front of you? Now I knew what Jazmine was bitching about all the time before she quit. She had just walked off the job, and her friend Karla followed her, meaning the last entry date on service point was months ago. I didn't understand it. Didn't the board see what was happening down here, or was Thrifty lying to them about everything?

The turnaround rate was big time with staff members. They hired a woman named Wilma. She had been kicked off the police force. Well, not the actual police force, but she was a community service person, a dog catcher. Wilma was a stickler for doing things her way and not letting anyone else do anything. She was mixed breed, maybe Native American or

African American. Her main responsibility as a CSO was scheduling. No one who worked with her on the night shift got along with her.

They also hired a guy named Lucas. His first night was on the overnight shift with me. I told him my story, and he shared his after. He was 25 years old and was from the south side of Chicago. His parents made it big in the stock market. They received a hot tip and went for it. He was just a child at the time. They packed up the whole family and moved to a town called Lona, Wisconsin. Just a few years ago, both of his parents were in a deadly car accident, and both passed away. He had an older brother and sister. They divided everything in the estate equally; now, here he was.

Well, I gave him the overnight checklist that night, and he did well. I helped a little, but it didn't take a rocket scientist to set up the kitchen and keep the laundry going. He didn't mind going back there and setting things up. He wasn't like the old staff who didn't want to do anything back there. It actually got a lot easier since the client laundry list was done. Even setting up the kitchen went much quicker since the night shift volunteer started fixing all the working client lunches.

I had time in the office again, so I set up the Workers' Verification List. I created another spreadsheet. When I first started, eight clients worked there at the time. We now had 21 working clients; the programs were working. I looked at the document that Bobbie and Bella set up. I typed all their names into the spreadsheet. On top of the spreadsheet, I typed in the intake date, the date they started the job, the company's name, phone number, the weekly or bi-weekly amount of their check, and the year-to-date gross pay since living at the shelter. I placed a copy of the pay stub in the client's file. I typed a note in the shift report detailing how I set up the workers' verification.

I knew from sleeping on the floor that some clients reported employment when unemployed. A working client's benefits included a saved spot, a wake-up call, and a worker's lunch. Clients had to bring in a pay stub from then on to receive the benefits of a working client. Many clients started saying that I was running the shelter. They saw everything that I was setting up. They even started asking me when I'd return to the night shift. I knew there was no way in hell Thrifty would ever put me on the night shift because, for sure, I would take over the shelter and run it how it should've been running.

The numbers at the shelter steadily increased since Raine left. We were up to 55 clients each night sleeping on the floor. The staff was upset and felt that Thrifty should do something about it. I had to train Wilma on the overnight shift. Other staff members who had worked with her had told me to watch out. It was her way, and that was the only way. I showed the staff the email Thrifty sent me: "Please do not put any personal information about any working clients at the shelter. The board members don't want to see this."

The staff loved the idea of the workers' verification. Even a lot of the clients liked it. They thought it was unfair for someone to sign up for lunch when they didn't work. Most of our clients had to go to the Salvation Army for a free lunch from 11:30 to 12:30 daily. I handed Wilma a copy of the overnight checklist after all the staff members left for the night. She just looked at me strangely. I didn't care if she came back there with me or not. If she didn't want to learn what to do, that wasn't on me. So I went in the back and started to do what needed to be done.

I did some of the work and thought I'd see if Wilma changed her mind about helping out in the back. When I came out, I noticed Wilma talking with a client sitting at the table. She told the client to lay down on the mat. I kept on walking toward the office. I knew that, eventually, she would be back in the office, and we could sit down and talk without waking up any of the sleeping clients.

Occasionally, I'd allow a client to sit at the table if they couldn't sleep, just as long as they didn't make any noise or wake up other sleeping clients and respected that rule with me. Eventually, I would talk with the client to find out if anything was going on and offer my help if necessary.

Sometimes, a client would ask if they could come to the office to talk with me. I had no problem with that at all.

Wilma sat down, pulled up the overnight checklist on the computer, and showed me what it stated: "No clients are allowed to sit at the table during the night. They are to remain on their mats from 10:00 p.m. until 6:00 in the morning unless they have to use the restrooms or if they're going to work. The only exception to this rule is if a client has an issue."

I knew Thrifty was the boss, but why didn't he tell me he changed what I had written up? How did Wilma know, and I didn't? It was only her third day working at the shelter. It came to me only seconds later. It was the game player, playing his little game. I left a note right under the note: "If there's a client sleeping on the floor at the shelter and they don't have any issues, maybe we should ask the client what they're doing at the shelter."

After I was done typing my note. I checked the spreadsheet to see how many clients have been gone for more than three consecutive days. I also checked the chalkboard to see if any clients had been calling in.

This process used to be performed on the night shift, but ever since Thrifty became the boss, he never trained anyone on the night shift on the process, and if he did, no one listened to him. Wilma walked out of the office as soon as I entered. She sat right outside the office door. I thought, *Something is wrong with this person!* I read what she typed up in the shift report: "Staff member Wilma and Jimmy had a disagreement about a client sitting at the table. Jimmy does not want to follow the rules set by the shelter with clients with issues."

I didn't know who this person thought she was. She was never homeless or even worked at a homeless shelter before. It was only her third day on the job, and she had problems with other staff members and now me. There were big red flags here. I typed up my own little note: "This is Wilma's first overnight shift at the shelter with me, and she doesn't want to be trained on the procedures. She chose not to help me break down client's bins."

I broke down a few more bins and worked in the kitchen. When I walked back into the office, Wilma got up and sat outside the chair. If that's where she wanted to sit, I was fine with it. I just closed the door and let her sit out there in the dark with all the sleeping clients. I added all the names to the shift report of all the clients' bins I had broken down and when they entered and left the shelter.

I sent the shift report off that morning. Thrifty wasn't happy when he received it. He called me down before I left for the morning, telling me to erase the shift report and that the board doesn't want to see this kind of stuff in the shift reports. I told him over the phone, "It's already been sent out. How can I erase it?" I don't know how he did it, but he erased the shift report that morning from his house.

Thrifty had never assigned anyone to work in the basement. A few months after Maxwell started, he went down there a few times, trying to straighten it out, but he gave up on it. I guess every time Thrifty would accept donations, he wouldn't put anything away.

It was almost a year since Klazina left the Shelter, and the basement was a mess. At the staff meeting, Dick, Thrifty, and Debbie agreed to get some extra volunteers to help in the basement. Dick also gave everyone working at the shelter a $1.00 raise. I think he thought that some problems would disappear if everyone got a raise. However, I knew that wouldn't happen if Thrifty was the boss. I just couldn't believe it. The shelter had a boss who wanted to stir up trouble in the office, where most bosses would want their staff to get along to make their job easier, but he had his favorites, and that was it.

Maxwell said that during his interview with Thrifty, all he did was talk about how he was some supervisor at a construction company. I didn't believe that for a minute. My father worked in construction all his life, and they never put up with someone like this. He would've gotten hurt on the job, just like Mr. Hoffa.

Before being pardoned by President Richard Nixon in 1971, Mr. Hoffa, the infamous labor leader, spent four years in prison for his crimes as president of America's largest union, the International Bothers of Teamsters, mail fraud, and bribery. Two weeks before Hoffa's disappearance on July 30, 1975, federal investigators discovered that hundreds of millions of dollars had been stolen from the Teamsters' largest pension fund. Their attention immediately turned to Mafia bosses Tony Jack and Tony Pro, both of whom reportedly agreed to meet with Hoffa the very day of his disappearance.

While the suspects and motives were clear, evidence proved far more elusive. Officials later admitted to hypnotizing suspects and witnesses to gather evidence against the Mob, but it didn't work. The FBI began its search anew in 2006 at a horse farm in Michigan; the investigation yielded nothing. Hoffa's body has never been found. The following night, I re-did the chores list. I did chores when I was living on the floor. There were simply too many chores that needed to be done, and motivating some clients to complete them in the morning was challenging. I kept the same chores on the list, but I combined some. As a result, clients started doing chores. The place started to look cleaner and cleaner. I even came up with the Sunday morning cleaning crew.

On Sunday mornings, there is a signup sheet; seven clients may stay late to ensure the shelter is clean—both offices, the lobby, all four bathrooms, and all tables. If more clients wanted to stay late to clean, they were not guaranteed a ride in the van. They would have to find their own way from the shelter. After cleaning the shelter, the lead person would drive the clients to the drop-off point. The clients liked the idea of the Sunday morning cleaning, as I knew they would. On Sundays, Wood County Library didn't open up for the day, so clients had nowhere to go. There was a nonprofit church that would open up, but that would be later in the morning. In addition, it was wintertime, so they could stay off the streets for that extra hour.

The workers' verification started up. I made copies of their pay stubs and entered the information into the computer. I unearthed that one client had been sleeping on the floor for 11 months, and his year-to-date pay stub was over $11,000.00. We even had a few clients who had anywhere from $3,000.00 to $7,000.00 income, sleeping on the floor. Some clients who were almost there for a year on the floor were even college graduates who stayed last year for nine months, came back only a few months later, and were back at the shelter for over a year.

Our numbers were almost at 60, so Dick and Thrifty hired another person. About a week earlier, Dick had resigned. The new hire's name was Clay; he was hired to work the 5-10 shift. I never saw the person. I heard from the staff that he was from a small town way up north in Wisconsin, a one-horse and buggy town and that he was a volunteer firefighter. Clay was also a woodsman into hunting, fishing, and trapping, which was how he made his living. He ran into a few bad years and had to get a regular job to make ends meet.

Thrifty thought that he would become the new director of the shelter. He would've been way out of his league if that happened. He sent out an email to all of the staff to see who was interested in doing service point.

I didn't acknowledge his email. I knew he wouldn't give me service point; that would be the last piece of the puzzle left for me at the shelter, and that would've bogged me down. I wouldn't have time to help the clients as much as I had been. Thrifty even told Wilma and Han that one of the two would be the next manager.

The night shift was just a big mess, and it wasn't getting any better with staff. Rubio and I would text back and forth about how we felt about working with Han and Wilma. The other staff members would also text about the same people. No one wanted to work with them. It was no big secret. They weren't good with the clients either. They even argued over how things were supposed to go on their shift.

Thrifty wasn't any help. When staff called him at home, he wouldn't answer the phone call. They would wait for him to call back, but nothing. Susan started to call me at home about situations at the shelter. Besides stirring up trouble and service point, no one really knew what Thrifty did at the shelter. He didn't do anything to help clients, and no one could understand why he went home at 6:00 when the shelter opened at 5:00. How was he training staff on shelter procedures? The clients even saw it; they would come to me every morning, reporting what happened the previous night. I just couldn't believe some of the things the clients told me in the mornings. I was their leader, and they knew it, but I knew a client would challenge me one day.

I came up with the 4:30 to 12:30 checklist so staff and clients had something to go on. I figured it would stop some of the crap going on the night shift with the clients and staff. The checklist is as follows:

The 4:30-12:30 Checklist

All staff members are responsible for looking at the calendar behind the office door to know the name of the coordinator or host/hostess serving the evening meal. The 4:30 lead person will assume multiple responsibilities at the beginning of their shift. They will initiate the process by unlocking both the main and lobby doors for access, followed by activating the computer and security monitor and unlocking the active filing cabinet to retrieve necessary documents. Also, they will review the previous shift's report from the overnight shift and assess any new intakes that might have arrived during that time, maintaining awareness of recent developments. Next, they will compile the client log-in book, listing the names of working clients by referring to the workers' list and the chalkboard in the office. The lead person will also organize the search tables for efficient use and ensure a hospitable environment by welcoming and directing incoming volunteers guiding them to the appropriate kitchen coordinator or host/hostess.

The 4:30 staff member will begin their shift by checking the coffee cart, ensuring an adequate number of coffee cups, sugar, cream, stir sticks, and related supplies. They will then wheel the cart out to the water fountain and plug in the coffee and water pot. Following this, the 4:30 staff driver will inspect the washers and dryers in the laundry room. If laundry is to be done, they will load it into the washers and dryers accordingly. The next task is to greet and guide any incoming volunteers to the coordinator or host/hostess in the kitchen area. Staff will review the previous shift's report and examine any new intakes from the overnight shift. Retrieving the keys from the office closet is the next step, followed by distributing the pre-sign-in sheet to clients outside unless the shelter is at maximum capacity, in which case, this step is unnecessary. Finally, the driver will conduct a safety check by walking around the van, log the date, miles, and destination in the driver's log, and upon reaching the pickup point, will call the shelter to inform the lead person of the number of clients present at the pickup location.

The 5:00 lead person will be responsible for the phone and shift report for the night. If a client comes in with a deadly weapon, they must pass it to the lead person through the security tray. The lead person will take the weapon, document it on the locker verification form, and lock it up before the client can enter the shelter. The lead person is responsible for supervising all new intakes and asking a series of questions. These questions encompass inquiries about their overnight location, future plans, income sources, and any criminal records. The lead person should collect two forms of identification from the new intake, make color copies of these documents, and then return them to the new intake. Lastly, the lead person will provide the new intake with a pre-screen form to complete for record-keeping purposes.

The 4:30 and 5:00 staff members are responsible for conducting searches for all clients, which involves signing in on the client's log-in book and, if applicable, signing up on the workers' list. Clients are required to empty all personal belongings, including pockets, backpacks, and bags, into a designated laundry basket. To ensure safety, staff members will request clients to raise *their pant legs to ankle height for a contraband check, and for smokers, their cigarette packs will be inspected. If a client needs items to be locked up, they will report to the office, where the lead person will document it on a locker verification form and secure the items. A few clients will be asked to assist in setting up tables and chairs for the upcoming dinner service.*

The 5:30 lead person will begin their duties by checking CAP, wants and warrants, and the sex registry. They will also ensure the addition of new intakes to the guest master and spreadsheet. The lead person will set up folders for new intakes, organizing them by last name, first name, middle initial, and date of birth (DOB). If a client is a veteran, the folder will be marked with a 'V' and highlighted in blue, while if they are a sex offender, an 'S' will be placed on the folder and highlighted in yellow, with the same notation made in the guest master and spreadsheet. The lead person will retrieve the pre-screen form from the client, have them sign all necessary release forms before entry, and conduct the intake process after supper. Once the searches have slowed down, the 5 to 10 staff member will engage with the volunteers, ensuring that dinner will be served at 6:00 and addressing any needs they might have. Lastly, the staff member will check the washers and dryers.

The 6:00 lead person's responsibilities include securing the lobby door and returning the search tables to their designated locations. They will also carefully review the clients' log-in book for legibility, and if any names are unclear, they will locate the clients, request them to re-sign their names, and then initial it for clarity. When the volunteers are prepared to serve dinner, they will make an announcement. Additionally, the volunteers have the option to offer a shelter prayer if they choose to do so. Ensuring that all clients are appropriately lined up for meal service and that the volunteers serve clients at the tables is crucial because it promotes self-sufficiency and responsibility in the shelter's operations.

At 6:00, the driver has the option to go home, and if they wish to stay for dinner, they are allowed to. However, before departing, the driver is expected to thank the volunteers for their assistance. At the same time, the 5 to 10 staff member will review the previous shift's report and access any new intakes from the overnight shift. The 4:30 to 11 shift person will prepare all the bins for new intakes, affixing a white label with the client's first name and last initial to each one. At 6:45, the lead person assumes responsibility for conducting all new intakes, although it is possible for a staff member to handle them if an agreement has been reached to do so.

At 7:00, a staff member will make an announcement to begin placing mats out, and everyone is expected to assist in an orderly fashion. The arrangement involves specific guidelines: the first row closest to the office is designated for women while working women sleep by the fireplace. The second row, reserved for men, should have no more than nine mats to allow for the overnight shift's food cart access for breakfast preparation. If the shelter reaches maximum capacity, clients can sleep in this area as long as they are awake by 6:00 in the morning and have their mats and bins picked up to maintain a clear path for staff members and clients. Rows 3 and 4 each accommodate ten mats. The last row against the wall is exclusively for working clients, although in cases of maximum capacity, staff members may permit non-working clients to sleep there.

At 7:15, turn on both TVs. If there's a movie ready to be played, go ahead and start it. But if there's a sport event, switch the channel to the sport event. The lights should be dimmed for a comfortable atmosphere. If a working client arrives and is signed up for a food tray, a staff member will promptly notify the volunteer responsible for serving the client's meal, ensuring condiments like salt, pepper, ketchup, and mustard are placed on the food cart for the client's use. Once a new intake is completed, the lead person must create a black-and-white copy of the intake form and deposit it into the operational manager's mailbox. This information is then incorporated into the shift report, including the intake number, the client's first and last name, date of birth, and the reason for their presence. The new intake folder should be left accessible for staff members to review and for the incoming overnight shift.

At 8:00, a staff member will welcome and open the door for the arriving volunteer. They should inquire if the volunteer has previous experience at the shelter. The staff member should provide guidance on how to sign in and give the volunteer a brief tour of the kitchen and laundry room. An explanation of the laundry procedure should also be provided. In case the expected volunteer does not arrive, the staff member should refer to the calendar located in the office behind the door. If necessary, an alternate volunteer should be called in, and all such arrangements should be documented in the shift report.

At 9:00, a staff member will turn both TVs to The Weather Channel. If the movie is still playing, let the clients finish watching the movie. If there is a sport event, let the clients finish watching the sport event. The lights should be dimmed. Clients are expected to have their mats made up by 9:00, with their designated bins positioned in front of them, bearing their names.

At 9:30, turn the TVs off unless the sport event is still on and dim the lights. The coffee cart should be returned to the kitchen, and a briefing should be provided to the volunteer regarding the setup of coffee for the next morning. Ensure that no clients are outside smoking, and the smoke door should be locked securely.

At 9:45 curfew, one staff member will begin preparing the clients seated at the tables for bedtime, while another will initiate a head count. Once the headcount is completed, they should cross-verify it with the clients' sign-in log, and this information should be documented in the shift report. Subsequently, all lights should be turned off, including the overhead light in the office, while the two lamps in the office are switched on.

At 10:00, the 5 to 10 staff member goes home. The other staff member does a bag lunch count for the working clients. Check the workers' list and the chalkboard to see how many more working clients are coming in. Notify the volunteer how many lunches need to be made up for the working clients. At 11:00, the overnight staff member comes in as the night shift member goes home. The overnight staff member will read the night shift report and look at any new intakes. Also, the staff member will greet the volunteer.

At 12:00, the lead person for the overnight shift will arrive to review the shift report and check for any new intakes. They will also bid farewell to the volunteer. At 12:30, the lead person from the night shift will send out the shift report, conclude their shift, and head home.

There it was! I set up the whole shelter on how it was supposed to run right under Thrifty's nose. He was just too busy starting trouble and trying to fire me that he didn't even notice what I did. A lot of the staff members were upset when they heard the news that Han started to do service point. I think all of the staff members asked for it. There were two things I was pissed about. The first was service point would be done on the overnight shifts. Han would be moved to the overnight shift for four nights a week— two with Maxwell and two overnights with me.

The second thing was when Han told me the reason why I didn't get service point was because I was homeless at one time. I wanted to beat his ass right there, but I knew better, and I wasn't sure if my being homeless at one time made a difference for service point.

That morning, I went home and got online. Finding what I was looking for, it took me a while, but there it was. Even a homeless person could do service point. If a homeless person were doing service point, that person couldn't record their or any family members into service point. This really bugged me all day. Thrifty hit a new low on this one. When he told another staff person, I didn't get service point, because I was homeless at one point. I didn't even sign up for service point. Regardless, I wasn't homeless now.

I waited for the shelter to open. Rubio and Susan were in the office with Thrifty when I entered. I asked him, "What in the hell is your problem? I didn't even sign up for service point, and you told Han the reason I didn't get service point was because I was homeless at one time in my life!"

Susan got out of her chair. Rubio's eyes were wide open. Thrifty just started laughing about the whole ordeal.

I stopped him from laughing in a New York minute. "Did you know I went online this morning and read the rules of service point, and it states that a homeless person can do service point? He just can't do his or any family members."

He wasn't laughing anymore and said, "I didn't know that."

Rubio got out of her chair and headed for the door as fast as she could. I said, "You don't even know what you're doing here. All you're doing is taking the shelter down with your little game-playing. You don't even know you broke State laws by doing what you did."

I had a deep attachment to the shelter, considering it my home for over seven months, making it difficult to leave. Still, I found a way to contribute by creating my version of service point, taking care not to include personal information like social security numbers and addresses, as those details were already in the intake file. Moreover, due to President Obama's enactment of affordable healthcare legislation for all U.S. residents, I designed an enhanced spreadsheet. This spreadsheet featured client names and included columns for the intake date, healthcare status, F-Set participation, resume availability, food share, SSDI, gross pay while at the Shelter, payee information, employment status, start date, company name, and phone number. It also tracked the date of departure from the Shelter and recorded the client's subsequent housing arrangement.

After that, I entered all the active clients' names and filled in all the information. I deleted both the worker's verification and F-Set programs, as there was no use for either. I had all the information on the other program. I left about 10 blank spaces to place the inactive clients on the same page. If a client entered the shelter, I added them. I copied and pasted their information into the inactive area if they left. If a client returned, I copied and pasted the information back into the active file and added the return date. I'd been doing the same with the SSDI Program since I started it.

There was a lot of good information. Most clients found housing within two months if they were on SSDI. But since I'd been keeping records, about five clients returned but found housing within two months again. One client was in and out and had a payee. It wasn't service point, but it was my version. I needed to get to the night shift so I could have more time with the clients and start to do goals with them. I would be doing what Raine did when she worked here.

Some clients were already enrolled in healthcare programs, as they were aware of the upcoming changes. However, a few clients did not have healthcare coverage initially. When they eventually acquired it, I documented this information in the shift report. After all, I was the one consistently encouraging and motivating clients to take these steps toward obtaining healthcare coverage. Thrifty had the same old song and dance in his email: "Please don't be putting in the shift notes about clients getting food share and healthcare; the board members don't want to see this personal information."

I replied to Thrifty's email, "Could you please tell me why the board wouldn't want to know what is happening with clients staying at the shelter?"

He never replied to my email. I started to run the program and added goals and the date each goal was accomplished. I started bi-weekly goals for working clients because it allowed me to meet with them before they headed to work. I also did goals for a few clients who were not currently employed. Maxwell and I didn't like working with Han. It wasn't because he didn't do anything in the back; we were happy about that. He treated us like he was better than us and was in charge because he did service point. He thought that he would be the next shelter manager.

Maxwell hit it on the head about why Thrifty kept the two around. The more complications in the office, the more he could tell the board about the problems in the office and how none of us got along. Different cliques formed right away on the night shift. It got bad when Rubio got sick and ended up in the ICU. The doctors didn't know what was wrong with her at first. She had a shot in the back about six months earlier because her bones were deteriorating. It was a disease that ran in her family.

At the staff meeting, I was a little upset. My friend Rubio was in the ICU. We weren't as close as we used to be, but we were still friends, and I was concerned about her and Tia. When I showed up that night, I noticed that Thrifty had left his email account open with an e-mail Debbie sent him about the staff meeting and me. All of the staff got to read it. Maxwell even made a copy of it.

I sat down and read the email. It stated, "Just between us, I want to mention Jimmy's attitude at today's staff meeting. Wilma even mentioned to me after the staff meeting that Jimmy was very disruptive during the meeting. I like Jimmy, and I think he's doing a good job at the shelter, which is why I'm asking you to talk to him about his sucky attitude. I'm not asking you to fire him, just to talk with him."

I couldn't believe how unprofessional Thrifty really was, but I knew Debbie would be getting an email about it. I emailed, Debbie. "Next time you think I have a sucky attitude, maybe you should talk to me and not a co-worker who doesn't get along with anyone in the office. You say I have a sucky attitude, but did you ever stop to think that one of my friends, whom I've known for over 10 years, is in the hospital."

Thrifty never talked to me about my sucky attitude. Instead, he kept the email you sent open on the computer for all the staff to see; some staff members even made copies of the email." Debbie emailed me back, saying, "I sent that to his personal email account. It wasn't intended for anyone else. I know Rubio is sick, and it's time for all of the staff to pull together. I just went to see her a few days ago."

I just didn't get it. Everyone at the shelter, including clients, knew that Rubio and I had been friends for many years before we started working here. As far as staff getting along, I guess Thrifty leaving the email open was a good start, and Wilma's bad-mouthing was an even better start to getting along in the office.

At the staff meeting, Thrifty said, "I forgot to close my email account that day." I had to add my two cents. I said, "I just wonder how many times you've kept the service point account open unknowingly with all that classified information."

The shelter took some time to hire a new director, but they ultimately succeeded and hired a guy named Dean. The first thing he wanted to do was sit down with the staff in a one-on-one meeting to get to know everybody and try to figure out the problems in the office. I never met the guy because I was on the overnight shift, but I heard from other staff members that he was a very short person, maybe five feet tall. He had short, gray hair with a mustache and beard to match. He went to college to be a reporter but couldn't hack it. He was married and had six children.

The day I had my interview with Dean. I was all set up to meet with him and had a copy of my resume. I even gave him a copy of the speech I gave when I was homeless and sleeping on the shelter floor:

"Good evening to all of you. My name is Jimmy James, and I want to tell you all how you have touched my life. But first, I want to tell you how I got here. By the age of fourteen, I was on a destructive path. I joined a vicious gang, thinking it would get me power and security. I never graduated from high school, but I made my name in the drug game with ease, making my living off of other people's habits. I quickly moved up in the ranks of the gang and was introduced to cocaine and the devil's drug: crack. When a friend I had given a line of cocaine died sixteen hours later, I was arrested and charged with "homicide by explosive," the first case in the State of Wisconsin where cocaine was classified as a dangerous weapon.

While incarcerated, I found God and promised Him I would never return to my old ways of life, no matter how bad things got. I walked away from the drug and gang life I had lived for over twenty-eight years. When I told my parole officer about my decision, she told me that if she had a nickel for every time she heard the story of someone finding God and going straight, she wouldn't have to work another day in her life.

The only place I could rent was a ghetto apartment that was being condemned due to bugs. I had no furniture and slept on the floor. I started to write my second book, *Snitches N' B*tches* which detailed about the reality of gang life. Somehow, even with my criminal record, I was able to get and keep a great job for just over two years. Then, a new HR guy introduced mandatory background checks, and guess what? No more job! I submitted countless resumes and applications with no luck at all. I even started to look for jobs out of state.

Shortly after that, I became homeless. I started living in my car and showering at truck stops. I was able to get some job interviews, but I kept being rejected. Finally, I moved in with a friend and his girlfriend for about two months, only to wake up to the police in my room, grilling me about a fight between the couple the previous night.

I did the right thing and moved out to get away from the drama. With no one to turn to, I called a shelter and was told I had to be a resident of the county to stay there. I stopped in at another place in a different county.

I got a meal but was told I couldn't stay there because of my criminal record. I continued down the highway in shock, unable to fathom that I might be unable to find a place to take me in. I called a shelter in Wood County and was again denied due to my criminal record.

I was exhausted physically and emotionally. My gas gauge was empty. I started to think back on my life, about how things used to be when I was in the gang. I had money and power. I wrestled with the thought of returning to the streets, where I knew I could make it, but my promise to God echoed in my head. I couldn't go back. I didn't want to go back. I took a deep breath and called the shelter. They said I could come in, but I figured they would be just like everybody else.

It was such a relief to get here and be accepted. They treated me with respect and dignity, and I felt like a human being for the first time in a long time. The shelter staff helped me set some goals for myself and encouraged me to keep going. I was convinced no one would give a convicted felon a job. Now, I'm on my way to New York to pitch my books to high-level directors and producers to see if they want to make a movie out of them. None of this would have been possible if it wasn't for all of you out there, and the staff at the Shelter. Thank you very much, and have a good night."

I even showed him all the documentation of what I had set up at the shelter since I'd been working there and told him that I'd started doing goals on clients. When he asked me about the problems in the office, I told him straight out, "Every time I do something good here, Thrifty cuts my hours or places all of this stuff in my mailbox. It's his way of telling me that I will be fired. I have been working here longer than anyone else, and I'm still stuck on the overnight shift every weekend for at least the last 4 to 5 months." I continued with the metaphor, "Imagine you required an operation, and you had a choice between two individuals to perform it. One had merely read about the procedure, while the other had studied it and successfully performed it, resulting in the patient's survival. Which would you select to conduct the surgery on you? He didn't like the metaphor and thought it didn't pertained to the shelter, but he didn't think it was fair for anyone to work every weekend. He also didn't want staff to type up any more negative shift reports on another staff member.

When Thrifty made out the new two-week schedule, he moved Han from all overnight shifts to all night shifts. Clay went to full-time on the night shifts. The rest of the staff, Susan, Wilma, and Lucas, had to do an overnight shift or two. Maxwell was done working at the Shelter. He must've told the truth about Thrifty, too, because, after his review with Dean, Thrifty cut Maxwell down to 24 hours a week; he had always worked 40 hours a week. He couldn't live on only 24 hours, so he quit.

I was still on the weekend shift for the next two weeks. I emailed Dean and added Donald and Debbie's name to it. "I didn't get any weekends off. I would like to be moved to the night shift to be a better mentor to the clients."

Dean responded, "I'm not even sure what you mean when you say a mentor at the shelter. I talked with Thrifty, and he said the shelter never had a mentor."

I spelled it out for him. "A mentor is a teacher, coach, advisor, and a loyal friend. When a new staff member started at the shelter, I thought it went hand in hand that they should learn to be a mentor."

I received an email from Donald. "Embellish success! Is it a big deal that someone just got a part-time job at $8 an hour? Is going two days without drinking worth celebrating? Should we be encouraging a young man who is going back to college after being in jail 12 times? Yes! Not only should we be encouraging when we hear news of small accomplishments, but we should act like it is the best news we've heard all day. By embellishing (exaggerating the significance) something a client does, we show we care about people at the shelter. More importantly, we are providing them with essential feedback that might help them stay on the right path. You have nothing to gain by being discouraging. You and the clients have everything to gain by being encouraging. Their small gains are your small gains. So, embellish away!"

Debbie emailed, "Right on! And I want to call out Jimmy James. I have been reading the staff notes, and he is totally 'rocking' in terms of talking with clients and making sure they have the resources to move on. And, when he writes something in the staff notes about an issue a client is having, maybe someone else will know about a resource that could help, so please pass that along. Together, we are the shelter, and together, we can make a difference in people's lives. That is pretty awesome!"

This guy was all mixed up, just like Thrifty. He even sent an email on the subject: "Well said, Debbie! Keep up the good work, Jimmy."

They rehired a woman named Annabel. She had worked there before when Raine was in charge. She had long red hair and a nicely shaped body. She was around 5'8 and 165 pounds. She was never married and had no children. The reason she wanted to work the overnight shift was that she went to college right after she was done working at the shelter. She wouldn't do any of the work in the back. She said she didn't have to. That's when Homer quit.

Homer had been the driver for the shelter since it opened. He had enough. There were rumors about how he wanted to take over the shelter. There were other rumors that he didn't want to work with certain staff members.

Homer was over 65 years old and around 5'11 and 200 pounds. He retired from the Air Force and had three children, all grown up and living in other states. The turnover rate at the Shelter was out of hand. Nobody wanted to work for Thrifty, and he wasn't even at the shelter half the time. All he did was make the schedule; he couldn't even do that right.

I went and visited Rubio in the hospital. I bought her a nice plant. We were still texting back and forth. It seemed like Debbie went to see her daily, and they had become very close friends. Rubio was being released in a few weeks.

Thrifty came out with the two-week schedule. He didn't even know what day the Pantry Run was done. He had been the boss of the shelter for over a year and didn't even know that the Pantry Run was done every Wednesday at 8:00 in the morning. I emailed Dean and Thrifty, letting them know that I wouldn't be available to do the pantry run if I wasn't scheduled for the overnight shift on Tuesday. Homer always did the pantry run, and now I was doing it. I typed it up so they knew the steps:

Grab the keys for the van in the office closet. Make sure the entrance door is locked when leaving the shelter. Do a safety check around the van. Log the date, mileage, and destination on the driver log-in sheet. Turn left onto Adams, heading east. Take a slight right onto S. Badger Ave. Turn right onto Parker Drive. Turn left onto Wood Road. Take a right onto Compassion Way. The Food Program is the last building on the right. Back up to the service door and open the two back doors of the van. Do not block the overhead doors because other people in bigger trucks might have to leave while you are there.

Walk into the pantry and meet with Mel, who will have a cart of food ready for the shelter. If not, help Mel load the cart up. The cart needs to be weighed, and the driver must sign for the cart of food. Load up the van and drive back to the shelter.

When back at the shelter, go in and grab one or two empty carts from the kitchen and roll them out to the van. Unload all food items from the van onto the carts and roll them back into the shelter. Place all new milk behind all old milk. Find the drawer marked marker. Take the marker and place today's date on all egg cartons. Place all new eggs behind all old eggs. Remove all old bread from the bottom of the freezer and place the bread on other racks in the freezer. All new bread should be placed on the bottom rack of the freezer. Put all juice in the cabinet marked juice. Put all the cereal in the cabinets in the laundry room. Put the chips away in the cabinet marked chips. Place all the peanut butter and jelly on the rack in the hallway.

Fill up a container with fresh fruit and place it on the food cart. The rest of the fresh fruit can go on the back counter. Place any other food items place in designated areas. Check washing machines. Knock down all boxes and take them out to the garbage dumpsters. Go park the van and put away the key in the office closet. Make sure the entrance door to the shelter is locked.

All I was trying to do was educate them on the procedure of the pantry run, just like how I tried to educate Kevin about how all money wasn't good money. Kevin used to work for me selling drugs. He was a fast learner; he listened to everything I told him except when it came to Brandon and Tressa. They were from out of town and would meet with Kevin every second Saturday of the month to pick up cocaine. I didn't even know he was still screwing around with the two; if I had, I would've stopped it quickly.

It turned out that both were known snitches in their hometown, and they brought a lot of people down. They were getting paid to work for the police, and because they got so hot in their hometown, the police sent them out to different locations. When the police had enough evidence against Kevin for drug dealing, they picked him up and charged him.

Kevin was making the hand-to-hand deal with 2 oz of cocaine with the two when the police popped out of nowhere with guns pulled. Kevin was just a young kid, maybe 19 years old at the time. He already had two strikes against him, and this would've been his third strike, which meant it was life in prison. He wasn't going that route. Instead, Kevin pulled out a .32 handgun with five bullets, pointed it at the detectives, and started to pop caps at the detectives. The detectives had no choice but to defend themselves that day. Kevin always had this saying that they would never take him alive for his third strike. He died like a true gangster that day. The detectives dropped him right where he was standing. They had no choice, but one thing Kevin did as he fell to the ground was shoot Brandon in the head, which killed him immediately.

Tressa met her doomsday later in a biker bar. She set up a biker who went to prison. The bikers had fun with her. When they were done pulling a train on her, they slammed her down on the pool table and stuck pool balls up her pussy. After that, they took a pool stick and jammed it up her pussy. She died right there on the pool table and was found two weeks later by a farmer out in his cornfield.

Lucas was off work for a few days, and when he returned, he wanted to get caught up on the shift reports; that's when he showed me what Thrifty had typed up in red ink in the shift report. It was about me using too much laundry soap when doing clients' laundry. I had all the staff laughing on this one. None of the laundry containers were marked; there was no scale to weigh the laundry soap. How did Thrifty even know it was me and not another staff member or volunteer? I guess this was my penalty for sending the email about how the pantry run was done.

I told Lucas that I was a supervisor for the Pig Palace down in Milltown and how they would send their management people to these seminars. I attended a few of them, but the one that really helped me out in management and the drug game was the one about conflict, anger, and emotions. At the end of the seminar, the person teaching the class held an apple in his hand and asked everyone what they saw. There was no wrong answer. Some people said a doctor, a teacher, the color red. I said a fish because of the worm inside the apple. His point was that everyone had a different answer, which is how conflict starts. After conflict, the anger part would kick in because not everyone agrees on the same answer, and then the emotions would follow. This is what was going on with Thrifty because he had the title, even though he didn't even have a clue how the shelter was supposed to be run. When someone tried to help him, the conflict, anger, and emotion would kick in.

Debbie sent me a text message. "Hey Jimmy, I just nominated you for the Courage Award. You have come such a long way since I met you."

My eyebrow rose with this cheesy cat smile on my face. This could be the break I had been waiting for. I quickly started thinking about the trophies, I won when I was a little shorty. When I was in the fifth grade, I took first place. My mother kept nagging my father all day to take that block of wood and make it into a car. My father and I eventually took the block of wood and made it into a race car.

It was when I was in the Boy Scouts, I had the fastest car out of all of them. I won first place in the Soap Box Derby. That would be the biggest trophy out of all of them. I won a few other trophies when I played football and baseball, but this was an award, and I wasn't a little shorty anymore. There had to be some money involved. Maybe it would be enough to pay off the car.

I texted back. "Thank you for nominating me. Is there any money involved in the award?"

I waited for the screen to light up. There it was! "No, I don't think so. The award is through the 2014 Poverty Matters Conference."

I just sat there. Maybe I was counting my chickens before they hatched. All she did was nominate me for the award. How many other people got nominated for the same award? I texted her back, "Thank you again for nominating me."

It was time for the annual service point checkup, and I had been informed about it both by staff and personally by Han. It was a big mess and arguably the worst situation we had faced since the shelter first opened. *The big ass game player played his ass right into a corner, and he couldn't bully or lie his way out of this one,* I thought. Things had taken a turn for the worst for Thrifty. He couldn't keep it together with staff. Han was fired. From what I heard, he was the fall guy for service point.

At the staff meeting, an argument between Susan, Dean, and Thrifty really got out of hand. It was about calling the police; if staff had a problem with a client getting out of hand or two clients got into a fight, they were not allowed to call the police for help. Thrifty and Dean said that staff couldn't call the police no matter what. Wilma just had to get involved in it all for some odd reason. I couldn't understand this one at all. Susan called the police on Thrifty, Dean, and Wilma and was fired right after the staff meeting.

Rubio returned to work, and they also hired a guy named Wyatt. Wyatt was a few years older than me. He was a solid-built dude, around 5'11. He was a kickboxer and pastor. That was a hard one for me to understand. He drove a candy apple red 1990 Harley-Davidson motorcycle. They put him on the night shift. He got along with clients and staff. I really didn't see him, only at staff meetings.

It was a few weeks down the road, and they still had problems on the night shift. Lucas started complaining that they had lost control of the floor and the clients had taken over the shelter. Dean and Thrifty disagreed. However, I agreed with Lucas about the night shift losing control of the shelter. Even the clients talked a lot about some of the stuff that was happening. Lucas tried to plead his case, but the two didn't want to hear it. Lucas got so upset that he walked out of the staff meeting. Wilma went out chasing after him.

They just didn't get it. When I was homeless, I would be downtown with the clients, and some of them would even say how they would come back to the shelter just to piss off certain staff members. That showed that mystery loves company. When Lucas and Wilma rejoined the staff meeting, I couldn't believe what I heard coming out of Wilma's mouth, something I'd been waiting to hear since I started the shelter. Wilma never thought in a million years that Thrifty would allow it, which is the only reason she said, "You just think you're so good with the clients. Why don't you come to the night shift, and we all can see how good you are with the clients?"

I knew it wouldn't happen, and then I heard Dean say, "Yeah, I think we should see how it works out."

I almost dropped dead until I saw Thrifty's face. His mouth just hung open, catching flies. He knew I would take over the shelter. Thrifty would try anything he could to keep me off the night shift, and he was back to his old ways with the scheduling. He emailed the staff: "I now understand that I should not attempt the schedule while sleep-deprived. I am making changes to the next two weeks as needed to meet your requests. Please disregard the previously published schedule. I intend to make the revisions in the next two hours."

Thrifty saw how the clients and I got along even better now. I had time to sit down and do goals on clients.

Two weeks later, the new schedule had just come out. Thrifty put me right back on the overnight shifts again. He really didn't want me on the night shift at all. He knew I would show him up. He cared more about his job than he did about the clients at the shelter. I sent Dean and Thrifty an email stating, "I've been on straight overnight shifts since Thrifty became the boss at the shelter. Eleven people started the shelter after me. Is there some reason why you don't want me on the night shift?"

Dean replied with an email. "You're reading too much into this. The plan is to get you more early shifts. Lucas is going to sub status now, so we don't have him as an option for overnights."

I replied, "No, I don't think I'm reading too much into it. Thrifty had me work the overnight shift every weekend for 4 to 5 months. I even had to come up with two different schedule plans so Thrifty could schedule the overnight shift better. Now for the other mistake on the schedule. I asked for Friday the 8th off. I even placed my name on the calendar in front of Thrifty for that day off. I see I did not get that day off. I will miss my niece's wedding tomorrow. I have documentation on this and will bring it in today when I come to work. I am starting to see some staff members being treated better than others. This is not how you run a company. When another staff member (Wilma) gets to pick and choose her hours, and I cannot even get to pick a day off, you've better start to think more about it. Since I have been at the shelter as a worker, I have come up with all of these ideas that I use to move a client forward: the worker's verification program, the F-Set program, the SSDI program, chores list, laundry tracking, Sunday morning cleaning crew, the overnight schedule, and more. I want my seven and a half hours on the night shifts this week, and I want off this Friday. If other staff members can pick their hours, how come I cannot?"

Dean replied, "There were several things on the schedule that several people asked about. We will fix them and get this all resolved."

I was totally upset about this schedule thing with Thrifty. I responded, "I'm not getting this. Is Wilma the boss or something? She gets her hours, but she is the one who couldn't get along with Clay, Rubio, Han, and now Susan. Even Susan called the police on the shelter. I want my five-night shift."

He sent back, "Please look at the revised schedule that Thrifty sent. I think you'll be happy with the switch."

Clay was gone; he had enough. He saw the same thing so many other staff members saw. There was no sign of any management at all. Maxwell was back working at the shelter because he had no choice. He was three months behind on rent and almost became homeless. He decided not to stay long; he said, "As soon as I find a different job, I'm out of here."

There were schedule problems again. Thrifty just couldn't do it. He wasn't smart enough to. I emailed Dean: "I thought the plan was to get me on the night shift. The schedule isn't even close to that."

He responded, "You are 100 percent correct when you say that. Both Thrifty and I thought you would be a good fit for earlier (night) shifts. Moving forward, that will be the plan. Thrifty said he swears he heard you say you wanted to do more overnights than night shifts, and that's what came out on the schedule. As soon as I talked with him early yesterday (Friday) afternoon, he redid the whole schedule and changed you to mostly night shifts next week, as you requested.

He changed several other things because other people wanted changes. With so many staff changes lately, it is difficult to do the schedule right now. In any case, the schedule is only for a few weeks."

I couldn't help but be amazed by how oblivious this guy seemed, repeatedly missing the obvious. I also couldn't help but wonder if he simply didn't like me. I typed and sent, "No, I never said that I wanted to go back to the overnight shift."

He responded, "On my honor, no one scheduled your shifts other than you. Thrifty is in the process of revising the schedule for next week, and you will have more night shifts. You have to pull yourself together and think rationally right now."

I was sick of it all. "Don't put this on me. Thrifty is just jealous of how I get along with the clients. All I'm trying to do is move the shelter forward. If Thrifty wants to lie, that's on him, but the paper trail never lies. When are we going to meet so we can solve this problem? I know Thrifty told you that he and I talked about this problem, but you are wrong on this. When Thrifty and I met, all he said to me was that I wasn't trained. None of the staff was trained."

He was just so dumb that he didn't even know it. Here's a manager saying no one is trained; he made himself look bad when he said it.

Thrifty emailed all staff: "We are actively seeking a replacement for Wyatt, and due to Lucas's reduced availability, we ask for your understanding during this transitional period. Remember, if you need to make a change to the schedule or cannot make a shift, you are responsible for finding a sub for that shift."

It took almost two months before I would get five night shifts. I started to do bi-weekly goals with the clients because the number of clients stayed at 60 all the time now. That meant that I had to do six goals nightly. The shelter was finally being run how it should've been. Some clients liked the goals; they wanted someone to help them and push them along. They even had time to talk with me about personal problems in their lives.

Dorothy's shift report started with, "A client called and sounded intoxicated one night. He asked to speak with Jimmy. The client said that he was drinking and driving…"

That night, Dorothy gave me the phone. It was only her second night working at the shelter. She was in her late 30s and was a pretty little thing with short red hair and big baby blue eyes. She never had any children of her own, but she had a live-in boyfriend with four little boys who loved her.

The report continued, "Jimmy tried to find out where he was. Jimmy repeatedly and emphatically told him repeatedly to pull over and stop. The client then began to state that he was having problems with 'his woman' and wanted to 'test out the airbags' in his van. He then hung up. Writer looked up the number on the phone's menu (because the client no longer had the contact number listed in his folder). Client was called back, and Jimmy got on the phone and convinced the client to pull over, which he stated he would. Jimmy mentioned that he would find coverage for the rest of the shift and offered to meet the client in person to see that he was safe. He encouraged him to think about his children. He sounded very empathetic to this writer and continued to focus on safety.

The client continued to state that he 'wasn't worth 'it' and 'just didn't care and that he was going to check out to see how the airbags worked.' Jimmy told him to think again about his kids and continued to ask where the client was at that moment. The client refused to answer. He promised Jimmy that he 'wouldn't do anything stupid' and then hung up the phone. This writer was present in the office for the entirety of both phone interactions.

The client called back, and Jimmy answered. The client stated he was in the parking lot and then pulled out of the shelter premises stating, 'I love you guys, and I'm going to check out my airbags!' Then, the client hung up. Because staff witnessed him driving and the repeated threats to his own safety, this writer and Jimmy felt that law enforcement should be notified. WCPD/911 was called, and this writer gave the client's information and a vehicle description. However, no plate number was in the file for his vehicle.

The dispatcher stated that an officer would be sent to check the area for the client's vehicle and do a stop and safety check. Jimmy then left, and this writer will stay for the rest of Jimmy's shift for him. The client called back and said he was pulled over near the airport. Jimmy came back to the office. Jimmy stated that WCPD was pulling up when he was leaving; he told them the details of the current situation. The officer asked Jimmy to stay in case the client called back because he had a great rapport with the client and could perhaps convince him to give his location and pull over.

Jimmy then got on the phone. WCPD was here during the interaction. Jimmy got him talking, and eventually, after several phone calls and confusing information, Jimmy got a potential location where he stated that he would pick him up and they could talk or hang out. The client gave several locations, as it appeared he did not know where he was. Law enforcement was given up-to-date info as it happened. They sent officers to apprehend him.

The client was finally apprehended by WCPD after over an hour on the phone. He was convinced after several hang-ups and callbacks to Jimmy to pull over and give his location. During the interactions, the client stated that he thought he might have 'run another car off the road' and that 'it might be more than one, even.' An officer was in the office listening to the conversation and notified other officers looking for the client's vehicle. He told Jimmy that he would get arrested and was correct."

The client did not know the shelter had called WCPD nor that staff was trying to get him stopped for his own safety.

It was a few weeks later when it all kicked off with a client. Rubio, Dorothy, and I were working that night. We were notified if the client showed up at the shelter to call the police. Dorothy typed the shift report, "When the client presented at the shelter, WCPD was called. The operator told this staff person that we could let the client in but not to inform the client that WCPD would be in to speak with the client and that it may be after p.m. before police would be there to speak with the client.

Before the officer was able to come to the shelter, a fight broke out in the food line, and the client attacked several people. WCPD was called via 911 by this staff person. As the fight unfolded, the client hit and choked a client and struck another before staff person Jimmy could intervene and physically push him out the front door. All of this is on camera.

The 911 operator hung up while this staff person checked to see if any clients were injured or harmed. A call came in from another client that two approaching clients saw the client in the parking lot smashing car windows.

This staff person called 911 again and was told that officers were still on the way. The operator said they were checking "the area." At this time, the WCPD arrived with several officers, and several clients gave statements. Additionally, those clients with vehicles were asked to check out the damage. Three clients noted damage and smashed windows and gave statements to this effect.

While all of this was happening, two clients arrived and also stated to officers that they witnessed the client smashing the vehicles, but due to being quite intoxicated, per their demeanor and their own admission, they did not tell the whole story right away, and police only took partial statements. This staff person called Director Dean arrived at this time and assisted the officers with the cameras and collecting statements from clients and staff. Dean placed the client on the 'No Trespass List.' He is not allowed at the shelter."

CHAPTER FOUR

COURAGE AWARD

I heard my cell phone ringing. I looked down at the lit-up screen and saw Debbie's name. I quickly felt the coldness sweeping through me. Debbie never called me. She always texted or emailed me with any shelter problems. This had to have been something big. I answered, "Hello."

Debbie excitedly said, "Congratulations, Jimmy, you won the Courage Award. They just called me and notified me that you won. I don't have all the details yet. They said that they will send me an email soon. They have told me so far that it's a two-day event from September 24-25th that will be held at the Wood County Hotel. It's free admission for you and a guest for both days to attend all the workshops. As soon as I get the email, I'll send it to you. I'll leave any other information I get from them in your mailbox at work. Jimmy, are you there?"

I wore that nickel ninety-five smile on my face. "Oh my God! Really? What is the Courage Award about? Did they say? Thank you again for nominating me."

Shortly after, Debbie said, "I just got their email: 'The 2014 Courage Award. In recognition of the courage you have shown in overcoming barriers to financial and emotional well-being and becoming self-sufficient. For the devotion you have shown to your community and others as a result of growing from your personal experiences. For your ongoing commitment to continue to achieve a better life and to help those around you in the process.' That fits you 100% all the way."

I quickly lit up a smoke. As my heart rate started to speed up, I exclaimed, "I still can't believe I won. Thank you again for nominating me. I would be honored if you would attend the 2-day event with me; you did nominate me."

"Well, it says right here that we both can have a guest attend. I'm going to send out an email letting everyone know at the shelter that you won the Courage Award. I'll email Thrifty, telling him to give you those two days off."

I checked my emails, and there was an itinerary.

Day 1

- 8:30-10:15 Breakfast Plenary
- 10:30-11:45 Workshop Session A. A1: A Woman's Nation Pushes Back from the Brink. A2: A View of Access to Health Insurance Seen Through Case Examples. A3: Common Communication Mistakes That Lead to Conflict. A4: Social Innovation: Changing the Paradigm for Addressing Poverty, Homelessness and Unemployment. A5: Debt Negotiation to Deal with Debt Collectors. A6: The War on Poverty
- 12:00-1:30 Luncheon Plenary
- 1:45-3:00 Workshop Session B. B1: Avoiding the 21 Biggest Grant Writing Traps. B2: The Criminalization of Poverty. B3: Ministry Dental Center: Growth and Challenges, Challenges and Growth
- 3:00-3:15 Break
- 3:15-4:30 Workshop Session C. C1: Local Strategies to Increase Immigrant Family Participation in the Wisconsin Heat Energy Assistance Program. C2: The Rural Front: Winning through Engagement & Empowerment. C3: Weight of the Wood County.

Day 2

- Breakfast from 8:00-9:00
- From 9:15-10:30 Workshop Session D. D1: Meet Your Mission with Advocacy. D2: The War on Poverty: What's New? What's There TO Do? D3: Workforce Strategies for Job Seekers and Businesses. D4: Finance is Fun! Building Financial Literacy for Not-for-Profit Organizations and Boards. D5: The Importance of Fathers in Breaking the Cycle of Poverty. D6: Community Conversations: From Small Group Dialog to Action.
- 10:30-10:45 Break
- 11:00-12:00 Workshop Session E. E1: Money Matters: How Community Action Agencies are Addressing Financial Empowerment. E2: Addressing Poverty in Families with Disabilities. E3: Why Poverty Gets Overlooked at the Capitol & How That Can Be Changed. E4: Economic Inclusion in Your Community: The Data and the Work. E5: How to Create an Inventory of Safety Net Clinics in Four Easy Steps. E6: Community-Based Approach to Addressing Poverty.

A few days later, I received an email from Debbie. "Did you register?"

I replied, "Yeah, I'm all signed up and will be attending all the workshops. It's nice that the shelter is paying me for the two days."

She responded, "You have a lot to be proud of, so keep up the good work! Just please don't let your anger about things get out of control."

All I was trying to do was explain what was going on at the shelter. I said, "Thank you, Debbie, but my anger is justified. I'm still working every weekend, and who knows what the new schedule is going to look like? It does not have to work like this. It really doesn't!"

She replied seconds later, "Well, then make up a schedule that gives everyone the hours they want and gives everyone (not just you, but everyone) every other weekend off. If you can do it, I'm sure Thrifty will be thrilled. He is trying, but if he gives people enough hours, they won't get every other weekend off."

This was the chance I had been waiting for to set up the night shift schedule. I already set up the overnight shift schedule; it's just that Thrifty wouldn't give me my weekends off. I sent, "Al had no problems scheduling staff. He had a problem with staff working together. Let me know the hours that staff can work, and I will make up a schedule. Thrifty says that a weekend is Saturday and Sunday. If you make a weekend a Friday, Saturday, and Sunday, one staff member could have a Friday and Saturday, and another staff member could have a Saturday and Sunday all off on the same weekend. This opens up the weekend, plus Wilma says she can work weekends. Even in my schedule, Wilma will have two days off in a row."

A few minutes later, she responded, "I would say tell Thrifty that you would like to try making out the schedule. Ask him to give you the hours people can work. See if you can do it. Are you saying you want Al back?"

I answered, "I'm just saying, I saw three people try to run the shelter. Some of the things they did worked, and others didn't. The scheduling was never a problem. Thank you for letting me solve this problem. Here is another problem that just came up out of nowhere. The shelter is down to two different kinds of cereal again. A staff member notified me that it has been like this for at least two months. Maybe email Wilma to pick up different kinds of cereal before she does the Pantry Run on Wednesday morning."

She responded, "Hey, turkey, I am NOT letting you solve the problem, but scheduling is hard, and I think if you tried it, you would realize that Thrifty is not being an asshole; he is just trying to make people happy. As for the cereal, I don't know that we have any options from the pantry, but I will ask."

I knew scheduling wasn't hard. Anyone who has been in management could make up a schedule. I replied, "I like that greeting, 'Hey, turkey.' The schedule is not that hard to do and make people happy at the same time. When will it be my turn to be happy with the schedule? I have been working at the shelter longer than anyone else and never get the schedule I want. Why is this?

When the new schedule came out, I sent another email to Debbie, stating, "I see that Thrifty used my idea for Fridays being part of the weekend for the overnight shifts, but I didn't get my weekend. It is just a game!"

Debbie replied, "Well, I'm looking forward to seeing the schedule! See you tonight."

◆◆◆◆◆

I nominated Jimmy James for the Courage Award. Jimmy has overcome many barriers and is now self-sufficient and working to help others find their way.

He was on a destructive path by the age of 14. Jimmy joined a gang for a sense of power and security. He never graduated from high school but did graduate, as he says, "into the drug game, with ease. When a friend, to whom he had given a line of cocaine one night, died 16 hours later, he was arrested and charged with homicide by explosive, the first case in the state of Wisconsin where cocaine was classified as a dangerous weapon.

While incarcerated, Jimmy found God and promised that he would never return to his old way of life, no matter how bad things got. He walked away from the drug and gang life that he had lived for 28 years. After getting out of prison, Jimmy found a job and an apartment, even though it was a ghetto apartment infested with bugs. Unfortunately, when a new HR manager found out about his record, he was fired.

Dejected and discouraged, he could have turned back to the only life he knew, but he didn't. Despite living in his car and submitting over 300 job applications with no success, he didn't give up. Trying to find work, he went to shelters in Fond Du Lac and Oshkosh but was turned away because he wasn't a resident. Just about at the end of his rope, he found the shelter, where he was told, "Come on in."

While at the shelter, the staff helped him set goals for himself and encouraged him to keep going. He found a job at Wood County Packaging, and after seven months as a resident of the shelter, he was able to move into The Salvation Army Project Home. During this period, Jimmy called the shelter and offered to volunteer. He felt that as someone who had "been there," he could be a help to those going through tough times. He spent many mornings volunteering for the 4-8 a.m. shift!

The job at Wood County Packaging ended, and Jimmy again was looking for work. Guess where? Right, the shelter! Jimmy started work there in February 2013 and has been employed there ever since. He moved into his own apartment last summer for the first time in four years! At the shelter, he works tirelessly to make sure all our clients receive health care, food share, and employment. He also shares his experience to help them understand that they, too, can get beyond their present circumstances and make a good life for themselves.

I have nominated Jimmy for this award because many people would have taken the "easier road" and gone back to a life of drugs and gangs. While there had to be many times that he wavered, he never gave up. He put his energy not only into working with people at the shelter but also into writing books. They tell of his life; he wrote them in the hope that reading them might change someone's mind about taking the wrong path in life.

As I stood there looking at the audience, I said, "First, I want to thank Debbie for nominating me, along with Donald and Josh, down at the Shelter and all their help and to all of you and what you do. Thank you." I received my plaque and noticed the audience giving me a stand ovation. I went outside to smoke. I was standing in front of the Wood County Hotel in my new dark blue suit coat. I called Thrifty down at the shelter. I said, "Hey, I fell asleep in one of the sessions because you didn't schedule me any days off for the two-day conference."

He started laughing; he thought it was funny. I texted him, and I spelled it all out. "Why did you think it was funny when I told you I fell asleep at the awards? I'm not coming in tonight."

Thrifty text back, "I laughed in frustration, as I just had to reschedule two shifts for tonight and tomorrow. Additional frustration comes from you not being responsible for finding a substitute to take your shift tonight."

I let Thrifty know how I felt. He had screwed up a big day for me and on purpose. "Well, if you would've talked to me before you did the schedule like a real boss should've done instead of always playing games with me!"

I received a reply. "I don't play games with anyone. If you want days off before the schedule is published, the calendar is on the wall. I take that into account."

I really didn't know if Thrifty was just this dumb or if he was playing one of his games with me. I pushed send on my phone. "No one knew I won the award until last Thursday afternoon, and Debbie emailed you on this."

He texted back, "If you are not coming in tonight, who is working your shift?"

"I'm a little busy right now at the conference. Why don't you call someone to come in for me?"

He said, "Because if they see the shelter calling, they won't pick up."

I just couldn't understand Thrifty's logic on this one. I never called the staff. Rubio and I weren't even texting anymore, so if I called a staff member, they would know it was all because I was trying to find someone to cover my shift. So what was the difference if it was the shelter calling or me? He just didn't want to do his job, and his only job was scheduling; that's all he did at the shelter.

I went online to check my emails. I couldn't believe what I just read. I texted Thrifty back, "I just checked my emails, and I see that you are looking for a replacement for Lucas!"

I just couldn't believe that Thrifty was so jealous of me that he fucked up my day. I read the next message: "I've called four different people today for both you and Lucas." As I stepped on my cigarette butt, I thought to myself that he didn't even make sense. No wonder the shelter was turning clients away. The numbers were hitting 63 to 65 a night.

I texted back, "Then why would you ask me who is coming in for me?"

There was no response to the text. I texted again, "I guess I'm going to have to leave what I'm doing right now. Thanks for the good planning."

As I was driving to the shelter, I started to think how Guitto, the captain of the Milltown mob, or Juan, the leader of the Tri-City Bombers, would celebrate with you when special events (e.g., birthday, marriage, childbirth, etc.) took place within their crew. They were happy for you, and they let it be known, and they celebrated with you. But not Thrifty.

I sent Donald an email. "This is a sad email for me to write. One day, I am being honored for becoming self-sufficient, and the next week, the schedule comes out, and my hours are being cut. I have talked with Dean and Thrifty about this. Dean said it's because I am going to the Grateful Plateful. I'm looking at the schedule, and there are two other days I could work that week, and none of the other staff are attending the dinner. Well, come Monday, I have to call food share and unemployment; so much for the Courage Award.

I am only getting 29.5 hours for the week. I have always worked five days at the shelter. I will be calling someone from the participant list from the 2014 Poverty Matters Conference to ask them how to send this award back to them. I will not accept an award that is not true, and I will let them know my reasoning unless one of you guys can straighten this out."

There was no response, so I sent Debbie the same email.

Debbie sent back, "The schedule is complicated, though it gives you an average of 31 hours a week for the next three weeks. Thrifty said in an email that he was doing a four-week schedule, but I only saw three, so I am not sure about that. I'm not sure what you are supposed to be working.

Are you supposed to get 40 hours a week? If so, you need to talk with them about that, and I would suggest having them (and you) write down what you agree on. As for the conference, I don't know what happened there. Unfortunately, they didn't name the award winners until pretty much the last minute, but yes, I thought Thrifty would give you both nights off for the two-day conference. I should have spent more time talking with him about it to make the whole thing work better. If they can only promise you 32 hours a week, can you find another part-time job to fill in?"

I was working hard on my books and on fixing up the car the repo man was looking for. I paid the publisher to re-edit, *A Line 2 Die 4,* and I had no choice but to make *The Melting Pot, Snitches and Bitches,* and *The Kid on the Block* into one book. It would be called *Snitches 'n' B*tches.* This was because Thrifty kept on cutting my hours. I paid for editing on *Snitches 'n' B*tches.* It was the three-book series. I wrote backward while fighting a long, hard two-year battle with homelessness. It was hard enough being homeless. Imagine writing a series of books backward. For the car, I bought four brand-new tires, a timing belt, a battery, filters all the way around, spark plugs, and wires.

I received an email from Debbie asking, "Did you ever send over any stories to Heidi about the Christmas gifts? She's looking for stories!"

"I'm sorry, Debbie, I forgot about it. I've been busy working six days straight and just finished an eight-day stretch. I worked with Dorothy Thursday, and we handed out the Christmas gifts to the clients. We will have something for you by Friday morning. Do you want one big story or individual stories?"

"I think some individual stories would be nice."

It should've been Thrifty's job to write something up about the Christmas gifts that were handed out to the clients, but he forgot to hand them out when he was working that morning. Plus, the clients were still talking about how Thrifty forcefully grabbed a client because the client was walking away from him when he was talking to him. I witnessed the whole ordeal. He did the worst thing you could do to a client or anyone; he put his hands on another human being.

A lot of the clients turned to me, saying I had to do something about it. I went straight to Dean and told him I wanted to fill a grievance about what Thrifty did, but Dean just laughed and said, "Why? It's not going to go anywhere."

For weeks, Thrifty had the floor out of control on this one. That's all the clients talked about. Some even said they would put him in the hospital if he did that to them.

I started to think back to the last time someone put their hands on me. I was in Walker's Prison. It was about a week before I was being sent to a minimum prison. This White boy named David pushed me from behind when I was in the bathroom. I guess some of the Hoovers put him up to it. They didn't want to see me go, and they were going to try to do everything in their power to stop me from leaving. Well, David didn't know it at the time, but Shock was in the bathroom when it all went down.

Shock was a hardcore biker from the Milltown Biker Gang. He was in prison for 14 counts of racketeering. He went to school with my sister. He kind of looked out for me here and there, just like the Tri-City Bombers. Well, Shock saw everything that happened that day in the bathroom. He wasn't happy, not one bit. He beat the living crap out of David right there and then, and after he was done beating him, he dragged him into the shower and made him get on his knees. David had to give him a blow job after that. David became his little bitch for years after that, and nobody could do anything about it.

Dorothy and I handed out the gifts to the clients.

One young man received pens, gloves, a hat, and a 10-ride bus pass. He shared that he would use the pens to occasionally write poetry and the bus pass to look for employment. The client said the gifts are "very useful and great." An older gentleman enjoyed his deck of cards, which he now regularly uses to play card games at the shelter during the evening. This was great because this client normally kept to himself; this allowed him to spend time socializing with others in a fun way. He enjoyed the big bag of pretzels so much that he admitted to eating so many of them that he "almost got sick." He is still having fun with the crossword puzzle he received and still trying to solve it. He was very grateful for his 10-ride pass. In the cold winter season, he uses it to get to the shelter rather than having to walk on the icy sidewalks and roads.

A middle-aged woman was very grateful for the pajamas, "cute" slippers, perfume, and lotion she received. She said she needed all of these items. She appeared very delighted and kept exclaiming, "So cute!" An older woman received some playing cards and now plays cards at the shelter. She said she received some good lotion that she needed. Because she spends a great deal of time outside in the cold, she states that her skin gets very dry, and the moisturizer was something she couldn't afford. She uses the 10-ride bus pass for doctor's appointments and to attend church services and a weekly Bible study. The client is disabled and said, "It was nice not having to walk on the snow and ice with my cane, but to have wheels."

A younger male client received a golf shirt. He really liked it. The client is quiet and doesn't say much, but everyone could tell by the smile on his face that he enjoyed receiving a nice piece of clothing that he wouldn't have normally been able to afford. It was great to see the pride on his face.

A middle-aged woman said she received make-up that she wanted but didn't think she could have because it was a "luxury." She lit up when she saw her new slippers, too. She wears the slippers each night while she does her crossword puzzles from her book. An older male client received a hat and gloves, which he wears. He also does the crossword puzzles. The client is a great guy who always expresses gratitude and offers everyone around him a positive word and a kind smile. Upon opening up the gifts, he enthusiastically said, "Wow, this is great!"

A working male client received long underwear, two pairs of socks, and a hat. He works outside, so the items were very needed, and he is grateful for being able to stay warm on the job. He used the 10-ride bus pass to get to work at his new job. In this weather, the less time he spends walking outside daily, the better.

A working female client said that she used her 10-ride bus pass to look for employment. She also received candy she enjoyed and a deck of cards she now uses to play with other clients. An older woman client used her bus passes to get to doctor appointments and look for employment. She also received a scarf and hat. She said the gifts were nice and said, "I really thank God that people thought about us." She was happy to let us know that while looking for employment, she recently found an apartment that might be one she can afford. She said, "Thank you for helping me find my new home."

Another working female client received a shirt, hat, and glove. She said the best gift was the makeup she got in her gift. The client is working and saving her money to move to an apartment. She was pleased to get a gift that was an extra that she didn't have room in her budget for. She talked about how it made things seem "almost normal."

An old male client used his 10-ride bus pass to look for employment. He said he should've not eaten the big candy bar at once, but the hat and gloves came in handy. He spends a lot of time outside and comes in each night with his new hat on. A young male client who showed up just a few days earlier received socks, gloves, and some candy that he really enjoyed. He is saving his 10-ride bus pass to get to work when he finds employment.

Another young male client just got out of jail a few days earlier and will use his 10-ride bus pass for school. He starts on January 19th and has been accepted into an accounting program. He was so excited about the school supplies. He said that the pens and paper would come in handy for school.

I received an email from Debbie stating, "Thank you so much for those wonderful stories! Heidi will be thrilled. I really appreciate all the work you went through to get them."

I already knew Thrifty would thank me, too, but in his way. I couldn't believe it; every time I did something good for the shelter, Thrifty penalized me for it. Dean wasn't smart enough to see it or didn't care what he did to his staff. Because I did the Christmas stories, Thrifty gave me eight days straight on the schedule. Maybe they like getting emails from me. I emailed Dean, "I'm requesting a meeting with you, Dean. I know a few months back you said no more meetings with me, but I think we need to meet whenever you get time."

He replied, "When would you like to meet? As I have said many times, all staff can meet with me whenever needed. When I said "no more meetings," it was my way of saying I think things are looking good right now. Anyway, I will be here tonight until about 5:45, and then I have a meeting at 6. Otherwise, tomorrow is open. I have a meeting at 3:00 p.m. Do you want Thrifty at the meeting, too?"

Thrifty scheduled me for the last five days of the week and the next three days at the beginning of the following week. I would be working eight days straight without getting any overtime pay. I replied, "No, I would like to just meet with you. Working eight days straight would burn anyone out. Now, because I called in sick on my eighth straight day, I lost a day of wages."

I don't think Dean took that into consideration when he changed our job titles at the shelter. We had these name tags that said Shelter, with Safety Manager and our first names. When Dean removed the title manager from the name tag, I was just a worker under State laws and guidelines.

He responded, "You can count the wages on your timesheet for today as one of your paid time off days, which can be used for vacation or sick days. In the future, we'll make sure you aren't working that many days in a row. I hope you are feeling better."

I knew now he knew nothing about State laws and that he didn't even go online to check it out to see what it said about eight days straight on the job. I replied, "I will not use my sick days or vacation days for working eight days straight. I want to be paid double time for the seventh day. It is a state law."

He replied, "We don't have any policies to pay people time and a half. We're doing the best we can to be fair to everyone. Thanks for working hard on the job."

A few weeks later, I attended the Grateful Plateful. It was a fundraiser for the shelter where volunteers would donate money. I gave a speech at their first one, but I wasn't a client anymore. They had a client all lined up to speak and tell his story. I sat next to him and his girlfriend. We had a few beers together when I asked him if I could read the speech he was planning to give. He pulled out all these sheets of paper crumbled up in his pocket. I asked him if Dean or Thrifty sat down with him and helped him write a speech. He said no. I went out to my car, got a few index cards, and tried organizing some for him.

As we were sitting outside trying to get everything together, we noticed the media coming in. That's when Dean looked over at me, placed both of his thumbs up to his temple with his hands opened, and started to wiggle his fingers back and forth looking at me. The client and his girlfriend asked me, "What is that about?" I told both clients, "That's his way of showing off that he runs the shelter."

Both said, "Everybody knows that you run the shelter."

There wasn't a standing ovation all night, and they didn't even ask me if I would want to give a speech about how I'd won the Courage Award. I knew I would have gotten a standing ovation without a doubt. It was only a fundraiser; why would you want the volunteers or donors to hear my story and how their money was helping clients at the shelter?

A few days later, I really wanted to know how much Dean hated me. I asked him, "Do you even want my donations from the books?" Everybody knew I was donating 10% of all my book profits to The Salvation Army Project Homes and back to the shelter.

He replied, "No, not from *Snitches 'n' B*tches* and *A Line 2 Die 4*."

I just didn't understand it. Part of his job was to raise money for the shelter, but he didn't want my money. Now I knew how much the man hated me. He never read any of the books. He didn't even know what my books were about or why I wrote them. All he did was judge a book by its cover, just like he was doing to me. It was either my criminal record or because I was homeless at one time in my life. What else could it be? It couldn't have been because I was helping the clients move forward in their lives, and if that was the case, he shouldn't have been the director of the shelter.

CHAPTER FIVE

UNPROFESSIONAL

Thrifty finally did use my idea about scheduling, but it was about a month later, so it could look like it was his idea. I set up everything right under his nose, and it was working. Ever so often, Thrifty would make a copy of the F-Set program. I don't know who he was showing the document to, but I was sure he was taking the credit for it.

I had all 5-night shifts. I remember how Raine used to have me sign my monthly goal sheet when I stayed at the shelter. I set up a bi-weekly goal book, which I kept in Dean's and Thrifty's office, where I did my goals with the clients. With the documentation on the computer and the goal book, it ran smoothly. I did nightly goals, and Lucas and Dorothy even typed up the goals into the shift report. They even did a few goals here and there. The night shift staff members finally started to get along.

The shelter was running well. We weren't even calling the po-po anymore. There would be a case here and there, but not how it used to be. Even some of the po-po mentioned how the number of calls dropped. Maxwell started helping with the F-Set Program and going on Craigslist to look for apartments for clients. He came up with the client rent book; he would update the book every two days. The overnight shift consisted of Maxwell, Annabel, and Wilma. They had problems on that shift with Wilma.

Thrifty still created problems, but not with just staff. This time, it was with the clients. The floor was out of control for months after this one. There was a client who used to sleep on the floor with me when I was homeless. He left the shelter but had to return when he injured himself off the job. He had to have an operation and returned to the shelter with a walker. One day, Thrifty got mad at the client as he entered the shelter and grabbed the walker right out of his hands as he used it to enter. Thrifty threw the walker across the floor. It barely missed a 7-month pregnant woman. It was just unbelievable what this guy thought he could do to people and get away with it.

Some of the staff went to Dean about it. He didn't do anything, nothing at all. Even some of the clients, the person with the walker, and the pregnant woman went to Dean, and he still didn't do anything about it. Thrifty had plans later for the pregnant woman. Instead of housing her months later when she gave birth, he called Child Protection Services on her, trying to have her newborn child taken away from her. That was his way of getting back at her for complaining to Dean.

Dean wrote a grant for the shelter, and it was accepted, but there was a clause in the grant. They had to have someone who was homeless at one time in their life sit in on the monthly operational meeting. I wasn't their first choice. Come on now, let's keep it real. They picked this person who once slept on a couch for a week over me. It didn't last long. The next thing I knew, I was at the operational meeting once a month.

A few weeks later, I received an email from Debbie stating, "The staff from the Food Share Employment and Training (FSET) program will be here to talk about changes in the FSET program. All staff are also welcome to join me at this meeting. (Jimmy James: please plan to attend the 3:00 p.m. meeting that day because that is your focus area."

Thrifty went right to work right on this one. He erased the SSDI file I had on the computer for almost two years. I had some good records of the clients on SSDI. Ninety percent of the clients staying at the shelter only stayed for two months. There was only one client who returned three times and was on SSDI. There was a lot of good information that could've been used to show people who wanted to donate money and how their money would help a client. Thrifty said he didn't do it, but I didn't believe him. No other staff members had a reason to ease the file. In addition, they had a backup system in case something like this happened; however, nobody could find the SSDI program.

Wilma was still upset that I was on the night shift. She never thought Thrifty would put me on the night shift in a million years. For some odd reason, she didn't think I could handle the clients. She thought I was too easy on the clients in certain situations. It was kind of like when I was selling drugs. If there was a man who spent his whole paycheck on drugs and his old lady started calling me bitching about how he spent his whole paycheck with me and the kids would be hungry because there was no money for groceries, to keep the peace so the bitch wouldn't go to the po-po or the kids wouldn't go hungry, I would take the bitch out grocery shopping. Sometimes, you just had to look at the whole picture of a situation and what was the best thing to do at the time.

Wilma was so upset that she even went as far as to start texting me at home after I left work for the night. I sent out an email on the shift report from home.

Debbie replied, "I know you're irritated with Wilma texting you at night. I don't know why she did it, but maybe she just thought of something and wanted to make sure you knew about it, so she texted you while she was awake. I'm sure she didn't mean to wake you up. But please remember that Dean has asked everyone NOT to put comments in the shift notes that should be directed instead toward one person. You should have just asked Wilma not to text you in the middle of the night. Would you consider apologizing to her? I'm sure she was embarrassed reading that in the shift notes, and I don't blame her. Apologizing could go a long way toward keeping things running smoothly and not starting a big war between the two of you. We need to get along. You don't have to like all the other staff, but it is important to be respectful. I'm sure Wilma is sorry for waking you up. Okay? Even if you don't feel like you owe her an apology, could you just do it for me?"

I was totally lost on this one. First, Wilma was supposed to be at work, so she should have been awake. If she wasn't at work, why would she be texting me about cookies and chips?

I replied, "As far as apologizing, I am lost on this one. What am I supposed to say? Sorry, Wilma, for waking me up two times in the middle of the night over cookies and chips? If anything, Wilma should be apologizing to me!"

Back in the day, we had a phrase for people like Wilma. We called them "telephone tough guys," which reminds me of this guy named Wayne. He was good for being a telephone tough guy. He would talk all kinds of crazy stuff over the phone about the Tri-City Bombers, saying how he would take the gang down if he didn't get his money back. I guess Santiago sold him an ounce of cocaine one day, and it was bunk. He wasn't happy about it, and for some odd reason, he thought I should get his money back from Santiago. He would call me at all different times at night, even sometimes over and over on the same night.

Apparently, Wayne wasn't keeping up with the latest technology. I went out and bought a touch-tone phone with caller ID. It would show the name of the person or business from which the incoming call was coming.

One night, Mr. Tough Guy called when Tony, Santiago, and Roberto were at my crib. The business name showed up on the caller ID. It was Stagger Inn, a club only a few blocks down the street. Santiago and Roberto split out of my house as fast as they could. I kept him on the phone, agreeing with everything he was saying. I knew the vatos wouldn't take too long to get to him. Wayne ended up in the hospital that night. I heard everything over the phone. I just wish I had been there to see his face when the two vatos showed up. They gave him what we used to call a picket fence. They broke his jaw, which had to be wired shut for six months.

The shelter gave the client a deadline to sign up and go to the other shelter, or he would be asked to leave. He didn't sign up and was asked to leave. He went to live on the streets, and it was wintertime. A few weeks later, he showed up in the lobby. He was sick, hungry, and hadn't showered in two weeks. I went out and had a heart-to-heart talk with him. He agreed to sign up and move on to the next shelter the following night. I even called Thrifty at home to see if it was okay, and he agreed.

Wilma didn't agree with the client being allowed back into the shelter for the night. She even went as far as to tell the staff that I would be fired within a few months.

She also continued to text me in the middle of the night. Wilma monitored how much a client was allowed to eat. She started to act like Chicken Nugget when he worked there. I emailed Dean, "I received three text messages last night from staff member Wilma, one at 1:54 in the morning over cookies and chips again, and two more at 2:45 and 2:50 on the same subject. This is not the first time she has done this to me, and this must stop! If there is an emergency at the shelter, I could understand being called or texted at this time in the morning, but not over cookies and chips."

I knew for a fact that Dean had no common sense at all. He replied, "I agree that the message should have just been in the intercommunication notes. In her defense, she is just sending the message while she is working and thinking of it, and it being a text, thinking it will be read in the morning when you get up. I never respond to text messages when I'm asleep because I don't know they were sent."

I didn't get it at first. He agreed with me, "but in her defense, while she's at work?" If she was at work and forgot about something, that was on her, not on me. It couldn't have been that important if she had forgotten about it at work. It wasn't that important to start with, and you cannot assume that I would read the text message when I woke up. My phone was blowing up in the middle of the night. Something I was taught as a kid was never to call someone in the middle of the night unless it was an emergency, like a car accident, if someone died, or other stuff like that.

The main reason is I was on the night shift, and she was moved to the overnight shift. That's what it was, and what did Dean do every night before he went to bed? He would shut off his text messaging but keep his phone on. What sense did that make?

Dean notified everyone that they had to set up a date to have a review done on them. I was all gung-ho about it. I added another column to the F-Set Program, Wood County Housing. Who knew where a client would be in 18 months from now? Maybe this way, the shelter wouldn't have all these returning clients for years.

Someone somewhere came up with the VI-SPDAT Form. It was another column I would have to add to the F-Set Program. VI-SPDAT stands for Vulnerability Index Service Prioritization Decision. It was a four-page document asking for all kinds of personal information about a client. When doing the VI-SPDAT questionnaire, we were told not to act like case managers and to mark the answer based on how the client replied.

As I started to do the form with the clients, I noticed that several clients scored low. It was apparent that some were not truthful in their responses to the questions asked. Not all of them were dishonest, but there were certainly a few who were. I didn't know what to think after the staff meeting on the VI-SPDAT, so I emailed Dean: "For the VI-SPDAT, Thrifty said when we first started doing them that we should not act like case managers. Now you are saying to act like case managers. Which one is it? I believe it should be done how the client answers the question."

Dean responded, "No, ask the questions only. Don't try to talk to them or help during the VI-SPDAT interview. At the staff meeting, I meant that if you know a client isn't being truthful (drinking, years on the street, etc.), check the truthful answer and not mark it the way they are saying it."

I could tell by his answer and how he treated me that he was dishonest. He didn't do any VI-SPDATs. I replied, "This is not how the VI-SPDAT was intended to be done by the person who set it up. The person doing the VI-SPDAT asks the client the questions and marks down what the client answers. This is how it was set up to be done."

I wasn't going to be caught up in some bullshit because my boss told me to do it his way. Look what happened to Han with service point.

I received my taxes back, and I had made progress on the books. I paid the publishing company for 2 Hollywood Treatments to be done. I also paid the publishing company to re-publish *Cement Pillow* as *Fracas*. Now, I just had to come up with the money to have an editor to edit the book. Thrifty kept on cutting my hours every chance he got. I already knew how the review would go for me because the two people reviewing me were Dean and Thrifty. It was no secret they didn't like me or how I was running the shelter.

Dean and Thrifty handed out this questionnaire a few days before everyone's review. When I was done filling it out, I wrote on the top of my document, "Without accountability, all that is left is haver."

I couldn't understand why they handed out the document with all the questions on it because, during the review, they already had the score marked in. I wasted my time filling out the document. After my review, I emailed Dean, "I'm the best you have. I have lived it personally and have set everything up at the shelter to move a client forward. For you and Thrifty to bring up my past at my review, I thought we were over this. I guess you and Thrifty just won't let the past go."

He replied, "I'm sorry you're upset, Jimmy. In your review, we intended to praise you for the many things you do well and note the areas where you need to grow. As I explained, you're doing great things. I hope you heard that message."

The message I heard was they were still calling me a drunk in my review. Dean and Thrifty called me into the office last summer for two reasons. The first reason is they wanted to know my address. I told both of them my mailing address, which was my sister's house. I used her address when I was homeless; that way, I knew where my mail would end up. It was my address for five years. When I eventually found housing, it was just a six-month lease, so I decided not to change my address. My sister didn't mind sending my mail to me. She even mentioned that this way, she could stay in touch with me from time to time to ensure I was doing alright.

I looked Dean straight in his eyes and said my sister's address. He opened the folder in front of him to check to see if I'd given the right address, so I said it again. Thrifty jumped in and said, "That's not where you live. There is no way that you are driving from there every day to come to work."

I told them, "This is my mailing address. Why do you need the address where I live? Are you guys going to come over and watch the Packer's games and have and have a few beers with me?"

Dean jumped in and said, "We need the address where you live, and if you don't want to give it to us, I'm going to have to let the board know that you won't give us your correct address, and you could be fired for this."

So I gave him my address where I lived. The second reason was about my drinking after work, when I was on the overnight shift. Dean said I would have to start acting more professionally because I was working at a shelter, and drinking in the morning wasn't professional for a person working there.

What was wrong with these two people? I was single, free, and over fifty-three. I had no kids or a live-in girlfriend and paid my bills on time. What was wrong if I stopped and had a few beers after work? I was still on the overnight shift, and it wasn't like I did it all the time. I only did it once in a while. I really didn't have the money because I had these Hollywood treatments done:

A Line 2 Die 4 is a cinematic courtroom drama with a protagonist who isn't a movie character but a real man with real faults in a frustrating situation of his own making. It has all the ingredients for an intelligent, adult legal drama.

Cement Pillow would make a very powerful feature film adaptation. If developed properly, it is the perfect kind of Oscar bait. Sexism, racism, and discrimination tied in with gang history and unfulfilled hope for a fresh start; this is the type of movie that the Academy eats right up.

When I did go out and have a few beers, it was always when I didn't have to work the following night.

I asked Rubio the next time I worked with her, "Hey, did you get an email from Dean about drinking."

She replied, "No, why, what's up?"

I explained to her that Dean and Thrifty were still calling me a drunk and that they scored my review based on my drinking. She just nodded her head back and forth.

She couldn't believe it, and I couldn't believe it either because everybody in the office knew that Rubio and Debbie drank together because Rubio would tell stories of them drinking together. It didn't make any sense to me; my co-workers could drink, but I couldn't.

My message back to him was, "A review is a reflection on how an employee was trained by the shelter manager and you. It looks like management isn't doing their job correctly for training! During my review with you and Thrifty, the topic of my being professional when off the clock was discussed, and we even had a meeting about this last summer. Could you please provide me with the guidelines for what is expected of me when I'm not at work? This would help me understand what actions are appropriate and which are not. Keep in mind that this writer serves as a mentor at the shelter."

It didn't take long to receive a reply. "You may do just about anything you want when you are off the clock. One specific thing you cannot do is form close friendships with current or former clients. Drinking alcohol with current or former shelter clients is also absolutely against Wood County Shelter policy. I was just talking with Thrifty and he said the shelter never had a mentor."

I didn't understand this email at all. So, I couldn't form close friendships with current or former clients? Everybody knew that Rubio and I were friends with benefits years ago. I used to sleep on her couch when I was homeless, and we used to drink beers together, so how would that work for Rubio and me? I really didn't know what policy he was talking about, and if there was a policy, how could I have signed something like that?

When Dick and Al hired me, I lived at Project Homes, another shelter. Raine and Al sent clients there when I was living there. We were all living under the same roof. What was I supposed to do? Ignore them and not even talk to them? What kind of mentor would I be, and what about Ava?

I was living at Project Homes when I met Ava. She was a young, pretty thing from Sweden. We were friends with benefits also. Did that mean I had to break it off with her? I'd met her way before I had the job at the shelter, and what about all the staff that worked at the shelter when I was sleeping on the floor and was now working with them? I even had a few beers with some staff members when I worked at the shelter.

What about the friendships I made when I was homeless? Would I just toss them to the side and say, "Forget you people; we're not friends anymore because I work at the shelter"? Dick and Al didn't have a problem with it. Dean just hated me that much. I started to think about the speech I gave when I was sleeping on the shelter floor. This guy treated me worse than my parole officer when I was on parole. I had to ask him a question to see how this all worked, and it seemed like every time I asked a question, he took it as a negative comment.

I said, "Please explain this to me a little deeper. This is a question and not a negative comment. I'm sitting in a bar drinking with a few friends, and a client comes into the bar. The client sits right next to me. What am

I supposed to do? Do I need to leave the bar, potentially leaving my friends without an explanation, because I can't disclose why I'm leaving due to confidentiality concerns?

Second question: A few friends and I have a party set up in this bar. We are waiting for one of our friends who did mandatory release from prison to show up. I haven't seen my friend in a long 12 years. I notice there is a client in the bar. Would I have to leave the bar after paying all of this money to party there?"

I couldn't believe his response. He said, "If you were in the bar first, I would just acknowledge the other clients with a head shake and then make every effort to ignore them. If necessary, you could explain the policy right to the client or clients and encourage them to leave the bar (Leaving a bar is great advice to give all the clients anyway). If you had to say to your friends, 'I believe there may be a shelter client here; could we go somewhere else?' That subtle break of confidentiality would be better than staying in the bar with clients present.

If the place is big enough and you can just keep to your own space, you wouldn't necessarily have to leave.

As far as leaving the bar, I don't think this would always be necessary, but strongly advised. Certainly, if you couldn't get a hold of the friend to tell them to meet you in a different bar, you could wait until the friend arrived.

Aside from the large pre-planned party situation, moving to another place in Wood County, a community with about 400 bar options, is pretty easy. Choosing places with little to no chance of clients or former clients frequenting is the best advice possible."

I replied, "Thrifty wrote on the review, 'Consistent relationship w/ staff and management needed.' Question 5 on the review sheet states, 'Staff person is not a team player or a trusted co-worker to front line staff and supervisors.' I received a 2 on this out of a possible 4. I have talked with

Dorothy, Rubio, Maxwell, Lucas, and Annabel about this. All have said they like working with me.

I'm also lost on what you and Thrifty meant by "front line" staff. I just about set the whole shelter up. Even on the bi-weekly goal sheet, it states, "The shelter manager and director of the shelter will do bi-weekly goals. Why am I doing all the bi-weekly goals for management?"

After that, I was done doing goals on clients and going to the operational committee meetings. They had this other guy come in, but he didn't last long either. Dean was taking grant money, and there wasn't even a homeless person in the operational meetings half the time. I only made a few operational meetings. It was like going to a staff meeting. During a staff meeting one week, we discussed the issue of clients' bins. Then, a few days later, at the monthly operational meeting, the topic of clients' bins came up once again. We didn't discuss how to move clients forward because they didn't know how.

The shelter rehired Jody, but he only made it for a few weeks before quitting again. He said, "Nothing changed here, and nothing will change here."

They even rehired Homer to drive and do goals with the clients. I didn't care, and I knew from the get-go that he wouldn't be able to do it. I showed him how, but he just didn't get it. Maxwell and Annabel were having trouble with Wilma on the overnight shift. Maxwell got so sick of it that he stopped helping the clients, like I did. He said it was Thrifty's job, and that's why he was in charge.

The talk in the office was at its highest ever. Some staff members were even saying they were looking for new jobs and would quit. None of the staff even knew why we had a review because we had already received a $0.11 raise for the year before the review took place. I started to play cards, dominoes, and a game of chess here and there with the clients. I still did my job. I waited for mats out before interacting with the clients in my actives for the night. The night shift staff had no problem with me doing it. As a matter of fact, they even said they liked how I was on the floor for hours with the clients.

However, one staff member didn't approve that I interacted with the clients. It was Wilma. She didn't think I should be doing what I was doing. I asked her one night, "What is the difference between Dean playing Bingo with the clients and me playing cards with the clients?"

It felt like I was back in prison, playing cards all night to pass the time away. The only difference was none of the clients were trying to cheat like they did in prison, and there wasn't any gambling either. In prison, gambling was against the rules, and you could get a citation or, worse, be sent to the hole. Even in prison, the guards treated us somewhat decent; they knew what inmates were capable of doing, like the riot that kicked off when I was in.

Moe and Curly were two guards who were very hard on many inmates and didn't even see it coming. All the inmates knew it would kick off sooner or later, and it did. That was one of the craziest days I have ever seen. Even all the gangs got along on that day. The main opposition was Moe and Curly. Anything that wasn't bolted down was being tossed from everybody's cell. The floor was littered with everything you could think of.

Eventually, the riot squad suited up with their body armor and warned all the inmates to return to their cells over the loudspeakers. A lot of the inmates returned to their cells, but a few hard-core inmates stood their ground against the riot squad and ended up getting their asses kicked big time.

They found Curly in the bathroom. He was beaten badly, and on top of that, he was bent over with both hands tied behind the toilet. He had been raped repeatedly. For Moe, it was much worse. He didn't make it through the riot alive. When they pulled his motionless body down from the razor wire, he had everything you could think of that was allowed to be in a prison stuck in his body.

I'm also lost on what you and Thrifty meant by "front line" staff. I just about set the whole shelter up. Even on the bi-weekly goals sheet it states. Bi-weekly goals will be done by by shelter manager or the director of the shelter. Why, am I doing all the bi-weekly goals for management? After that I was done, done doing bi-weekly goals on clients and done going to the operational committee meetings too. They had this other guy come in, but he didn't last long either. Dean was taking grant money and there wasn't even a homeless person on the operational meetings half the time. I only made a few operational committee meetings. It was like going to a staff meeting. One week at a staff meeting we talked about clients bins and a few days later at the monthly operational meetings there we were talking about client's bins. We never talked about how to move a client forward, because Dean and Thrifty isn't know how.

A few months passed when Donald and Josh asked me to come back to the operational meeting. They wanted me to start doing goals again and set up the F-Set program. They also wanted me to train all the staff on the F-Set program and goals. You should've seen Thrifty's and Dean's faces when they asked me to start up again. I knew it wouldn't be good, and it wasn't. I sent Donald an email about what was happening. It didn't take long before Dean emailed me on the subject.

He wrote, "Donald shared the email you wrote to him (below). You were off base with your concerns about last night. I was there during the whole time that you referenced. I was pleased that Thrifty was playing Scrabble with clients. We were all fully engaged in the activities of last night. You're doing a great job with client interaction, goals, and getting clients motivated to work and move on, but you have to stop looking for reasons to be angry with Thrifty. I am fully aware of how he is doing his job and am pleased with his performance."

Dean was happy with Thrifty's performance! What did he do at the shelter? He didn't set anything up or work with any clients to move them forward. He only did service point and scheduling after I showed him how to schedule. They even had to hire Matthew, a Wood County Shelter case manager, to come in every morning for a few hours to start working with clients. Matthew was a few years older than me. He was married with three children. He had been a case manager for 15 years at Wood County Shelter. Matthew would go out to the clubs occasionally and have a few beers. I remember one time when I was homeless, he was out just having a good time out in one of the clubs. I didn't know him then, but a homeless friend told me he was the case manager at Wood County Shelter.

Matthew knew all the ins and outs of moving a client forward, but there were two things I couldn't understand. He could drink with clients, and I couldn't. It was big news at the shelter. Matthew went out to a club while working for the shelter and drank with clients. The clients were talking about it big time. Dean and Thrifty didn't say anything to him about it.

The second thing was I would leave a copy of the workers' verification in his mailbox every week, thinking maybe it would help him out with some of the working clients. One day, I was down at the shelter early in the morning to do the pantry run, and I asked, "Is the workers' verification that I have been leaving in your mailbox helping you out any?"

He looked at me strangely and said, "I never received anything like that, but it would be helpful."

The first thought that came to my mind was that either Dean or Thrifty was taking it out of his mailbox for some odd reason. Dean and Thrifty didn't want bosses at any other shelters to know what I was doing. It would make them look bad. Maxwell hit it right on the head when he said, "They're the face of the shelters, and no one else could be the face of the shelter."

I decided to stop doing goals again. It didn't seem like my responsibility, and I wasn't being compensated for it nor given a specific title for it. It was the shelter manager's or director's job to do goals. I responded, "I never said you weren't there all night. Did I miss something here? I used to play cards with the clients, but Donald and Josh asked me to do goals at the operational meeting because someone has to do goals with the clients. This has always been the way the shelter operates. So, what happened here? I do goals so the shelter manager has time to play games with the clients? I see that you only addressed part of the email that Donald read. What did they say about the staff member walking off the job?"

He replied quickly, "I will address your points one by one. I was at the shelter to make the point that I didn't have a problem with him playing Scrabble with clients. I am his supervisor, not you. That is the end of that. Donald and Josh are not your supervisors, and they do not purport to be. We appreciate your diligence with the goals process. As you know, all staff will be doing goals, and other staff have been doing goals. It is up to Thrifty and me to make sure this is happening, and we will do so. There weren't any other staff members doing goals. They would type up the goals I did that night and initial their names.

Staff walking off the job is not your concern, especially when you are not working when a staff person leaves their job at the shelter. If Thrifty or I wanted to bring that concern to the board, we would have done so. If there was a concern with you during a work shift, I don't believe you would find it appropriate for another staff person, whom you were not even working with that night, to bring it to the board.

Of course, it is your right to bring whatever you want to the board, but, as you can see, they are likely to relay the messages to me so I can follow up."

My fingers were busy on this reply, and then I clicked send. "My other concern is why am I on the operational committee? I know you said I was off base when I sent Donald an email with my concerns. If I am going to be part of an operational committee, I think I should have a say in the operations! I would think this is the reason why I am on the committee! Please let me know because if I do not have a say, I won't show up. Why would I?"

He replied, "As I said, you are free to comment on whatever you'd like at any time. Everyone on the operations committee is charged with making the shelter as great as possible. I just didn't think your comments about him were in that spirit."

<hr>

The overnight shift was just out of hand with Wilma. Annabel told me she was looking for another job, and Maxwell told me he'd be done if Thrifty and Dean didn't do something about Wilma. I had to email Debbie about everything that was going on in the office. Two people on the overnight shift were leaving soon, and the shelter didn't know about it. I didn't even know why I tried. She sent me an email calling me a drunk. It was unbelievable why they just kept on calling me a drunk. Where were they getting their information from? Someone was obviously lying about me to them.

I was totally pissed off about that email. Here it is, a co-worker calling me a drunk. I replied, "I haven't had anything to drink in weeks. I've been spending my money on my books."

She replied, "Good for you. I have nothing against drinking; I do enough of it myself. But you can't do it if it gets you in trouble. We sure see enough of that at the shelter. Just please remember what I said next time you get mad about something, and think before you speak, or in your case, email!"

Debbie emailed all the staff: "There are rumors flying around about people being unhappy with their jobs. I hear some, but not all. Every one of you has a difficult job. I know that I just find the volunteers. I don't have to deal with drunken clients and people fighting or pushing each other or swearing at me (though I do clean toilets, just so you know! And I do laundry and clean the kitchen). I've been here since 2011, and this is the most stable staff we've had. And all of you are really great! And all of you care so much about every client at the shelter.

So, here's my request, and you can ignore it if you want, but I hope you won't. If you are unhappy with something about your job, please talk with Thrifty or Dean. They are both very good, kind people who do the best they can, and both of them will admit they are far from perfect. If you feel you are not being heard by either of them, talk to someone on the board. Any board member will be willing to listen to you. Please do not spread rumors about someone quitting or wanting to quit. That just gets everyone worked up.

Secondly, please try to get along. Every person here has strengths and weaknesses. If someone does something that upsets you, please go to them directly and tell that person nicely why you are upset. PLEASE don't tell everyone else! Many of us come from dysfunctional families, and in some ways, this is a family. We can be functional or dysfunctional; it's up to all of us. The reason we are all here is to provide shelter to people who are homeless, and I don't think there's a tougher job out there. I love this place, and I believe we can be awesome. I also believe every one of you shares this with me."

Lucas came back to work at the shelter. He couldn't find another job, so he had no choice but to return. He really didn't want to with those two knuckleheads still in charge. Annabel's two weeks' notice was up, and she left. She found another job that was about a 45-minute ride one way. Maxwell walked off the job for the second time. He was done. No one was listening to him about the complaints about Wilma from the clients and staff.

I sent Debbie an email, telling her how the shelter was going down because no one in charge was listening to the complaints from staff. She responded, "Okay, here's my thing. You stayed here, and you know that it provides a safe place for people who are in desperate circumstances. Now, you seem to want the shelter to 'go down.' That's what you said. Why?

Maybe you are unhappy, and if so, I get that. Nobody is happy all the time. You don't like Thrifty? Okay! But you like Dean, right? And you like me? Then what the hell is going on, and what can we do to fix it? We need to be here for people who have nowhere else to go. I have said in many speeches that you told us we were there for you when you were ready to give up. We still are. Please don't try to bring this place down. Please help us figure out what is going on and help us fix it.

Dean has said many times that you are so good with clients, and he appreciates you so much. That's good because you have done things a couple of times that make even ME want to fire you! And I like you! Please, Jimmy, be on the side of us, the people who want to help."

My fingers were busy typing a response to her email. Did she ever stop to think why Thrifty and I didn't get along? As far as Dean, that man just straight-up hated me. I replied, "Well, you got things mixed up like always. I never said I was going to take the shelter down! Where would you even come up with something like this? I said that if you allow Wilma to run around this shelter treating staff, clients, and volunteers like this, the shelter will go down. Rumors are not rumors when the facts happen. Now, do not ever threaten to fire me again. This is not the first time you have written an email to me saying the same thing about me being fired."

She responded, "You did say that. You said, "This place is going down!" I remember it, and you said it after you got mad the last time. I never threatened you with being fired. I have told you a couple of times that you did stuff that could get you fired, and I asked you to please stop because I don't want that to happen. I am not your boss; you know that, so I will never threaten you in any way. Geez, whose side do you think I'm on? I have been on your side forever, and you'd better know that. I am just asking that you please try to help this situation, not make it worse. Nobody threatens anyone around here, and nobody ever will. If people aren't happy, they need to tell Dean and Thrifty and let them know why. Nothing will change unless people are honest and open about what is happening."

She hit it right on the head. The two people who weren't being open and honest were the two bosses. It was like the truce between Guitto, a capo for the Milltown mob, and Stacks, the leader of a Black gang called the Hoovers, which happened a few years earlier. When I heard about it, I knew it wouldn't last long. Even between the Italian mob, most truce didn't last long. Two Step Frankie, a capo for the Pisano New York mob, warned Guitto that it wouldn't work out. They were at war for years, gunning each other down on the streets and clubs. I guess Guitto had enough of it and agreed to set up a sit-down with Stacks. At the sit-down, everything was all cool between the two, and the war between the two gangs was over. Guitto didn't know it at the time, but this was Stacks' distraction to get back at Guitto and the mob.

Stacks planned it pretty well. About six months into the truce, Stacks sent a few of his "everybody killers" after Guitto. It all went down at Jack DeSalvo's restaurant. Guitto was so relieved that the war was all over that his guard was down. He even invited the two EBKs sent to kill him to sit down and join him for dinner. When they finished eating dinner, they made their move on Giutto. He didn't even know what hit him. One person cut his throat, and the other person stuck two forks into his eyes. It was over within seconds, the truce was off, and the war started again.

I replied, "I did not say I was taking the place down! I do not know why you always say I'm mad. I do not get mad; I get upset. What you call rumors turn into facts. Here is another rumor that is going to turn into a fact. Two more people are leaving."

She sent back, "I was kidding about the firing. Sorry. You know I want you to stay, and I have not taken Wilma's side. I just said that Dean had asked many times that people not write things in the shift notes about any other staff, so you shouldn't have done it. He's the boss and a good boss, so I think it's important to do what he asks. It's better for everyone if people don't write things about others that everyone can read.

Wilma was back to her old tricks again, texting me about cookies and chips at one o'clock in the morning.

The email continued, "Wilma shouldn't have texted you in the middle of the night either. But that is not taking her side. She said I took your side, so I give up. All I'm asking is that you encourage people to tell Dean and/ or Thrifty what is wrong and why they are unhappy if they come to you about an issue. You laughed about people quitting. Do you really think it's funny? Cause I don't. What happens to the homeless people who need us if everyone ups and quits?"

The shelter continued going through the hiring process repeatedly; it never stopped. Debbie's email made no sense. Some of us came from dysfunctional families. Everybody came from a dysfunctional family in one way or another; that is just how it is. Even in the gang, we all came from dysfunctional families, but we all got along, and why? Because we knew better than to lie to Juan, and if we had to, we knew not to involve anyone else in the lie because there could be repercussions that wouldn't be good.

That was the whole problem wrapped up in a nutshell. The two bosses were liars! Thrifty was still cutting my hours and placing stuff in my mailbox at work.

Dorothy said one night, "People are going to lie to save their jobs."

The statement was true, but you could only lie for so long before the higher-ups would have enough of it and recognize what was happening. This applied not only to gangs but also to any organization or company. She just didn't get it. Why would I think it was funny, and if I did, why would I be running around the shelter doing all of these goals on clients?

I replied, "No, it's not funny, and I'm not laughing. Where you got that from, I have no idea. All of the former and present staff have told Dean and also you about Wilma, and now I see that Wilma has posted my name in the shift notes for everyone to see!

Now, you ask how we can fix the problem. You need to fire Wilma; she is the problem. Wilma will not stop until she is the boss, and she has said this several times. I know for a fact that I told you this, but you do not want to believe me for some odd reason. Something I did not understand just came to me. SIDES? There is the whole problem in one word. This is not a competition, is it? Were people taking SIDES?"

Even Rubio had turned against me. I sent her a text about taking sides at the shelter. She responded, "Yeah, that isn't right." A few hours later, I sent another text to her. Within seconds, I couldn't believe the text she sent me: "Yeah, James is blowing up my phone with text messages. I'll send a few over to you."

I was shocked! I didn't know what to think. I received another text from her within seconds. "I got lost. WTF!"

She had meant to send the first text to Debbie but accidentally sent it to me.

One day, I talked with my landlord and set up this client, a husband and wife staying at the shelter, with an apartment. Yeah, I started to house clients. It was Thrifty's job, and he wasn't happy with it. I was doing it all now. I even started hooking up with other landlords for other clients.

There it was; the publisher just emailed me. *A Line 2 Die 4* was done and ready to go live. I finally did it. I had a book that I was proud of. Shit! I was an author. I called the publisher to see how they were doing on *Snitches 'n' B*tches*. They informed me that they were in the editing process. I told them when they were done with the editing, *Fracas* would be next for editing. They asked how I was doing on *Sinister*. I was almost done with *Sinister* and told them I would send it to them as soon as I was done with the book. I was flying high until three days later when a client who'd been in and out of the shelter since I slept on the floor showed up.

Dorothy typed up the shift report: "Staff asked him to wait in the lobby. He became upset. When he came into the office, he began to swear at staff and complain. We tried to redirect the conversation, and he continued to engage staff in a very confrontational and demeaning manner. He was told he had to leave at that point. He walked out of the office and turned and said to Jimmy, 'Go ahead and kick me out, you faggot, with your speech impediment!' Then he said he was going to kick someone's ass and told Jimmy, 'Suck my dick, you prison faggot.'

The client was ushered out the door, where he began to engage several clients walking up the walkway in a physical manner and screaming at them. Staff called 911. They stopped him on the viaduct, walking, and told him he was not allowed back on the premises. WPD was helpful and said that if he presents again without prior consent from staff/management, feel free to call them, as they are familiar with the client and have had interactions in the past.

As the writer was typing this, the client called twice and once talked to James and once to me. He said, 'They can look, but they won't find me!' He then laughed and hung up. I stated that if he calls again, WPD will be called for harassing staff.

I called Dean the following day and told him I needed the day off. Dean replied, "I read the shift report from last night; it sounded like you had a rough night."

I shared that I had a sleepless night, tossing and turning as a flood of emotions overwhelmed me. I also opened up about my speech impediment. I went on about how my parents spent their living savings on doctors' bills and had to bring me home from the hospital to care for me. I ended up being quarantined in the downstairs bedroom for over a year. My father had to put a lock on the outside of the door and nail both widows shut because I wouldn't stay in the room. I had double pneumonia. My parents couldn't afford for me to spread my disease to my sister and brother.

I heard my phone ringing; it was Dean. He wanted me to come down to the shelter for a meeting to discuss moving the shelter forward. I sat there for a few seconds, thinking about what he had just said to me. I called him back, got his answering machine, and left a message, "What do you mean about moving the Shelter forward?"

When I got out of the shower, I heard my phone going off. I had a new message from Dean: "I can't say much about the meeting, but Thrifty is going to be at the meeting."

I walked into the shelter to meet with Thrifty and Dean. They asked me to step into the back office. That's when I noticed Josh sitting there. Dean said, "Yeah, we talked about it, and we agree that you will be fired for being unprofessional."

My first thought was to get out of the chair and beat the living crap out of Dean, just like how it was when I was in grade school when people made fun of my speech impediment. I had told Dean something in confidence that many people didn't know, and here he was, firing me for it.

I said, "Here you go!" I took the keys for the shelter off my key ring. "I guess there isn't anything to talk about. See you later. As I started to leave the office, I heard Josh say, "Jimmy, come back in here; I want to talk with you."

I walked back into the office. Josh said, "You need to sit down and listen to me for a second. You are going to need references when looking for employment."

I turned and looked at Dean and Thrifty standing there. I asked, "From who? These two people?" as I pointed at them. "Why would they give me a good reference? They don't even like me."

Josh nodded his silver-gray hair, motioning for the two to leave. He said, "Your services are not required here anymore, but we want you to resign. Now, have a seat so we can talk things out."

Josh wanted to give me some money, but the only way I would've taken money was if it was enough to fix my speech impediment. I wasn't having it. There was no way in hell that these two clowns walked all over me and talked all kinds of crazy shit about me, dragging my last name through the mud, and now you wanted to throw some money at me and tell me to wipe myself clean and get the fuck out of here. They had me mixed up like a can of mixed nuts. I said, "No, you can keep your money; I'll take my chance with unemployment."

When I went home, I opened my computer to search online for employment. To my disbelief, I found an email from the shelter announcing my termination to all staff members. Dean was in such a hurry to notify staff that I was fired that he couldn't even remove my name from the list of staff members.

Printed in the United States
by Baker & Taylor Publisher Services